Praise for Jackie and Doug

You have to wonder if those poking fun consider for even a moment that in the world of professional athletes—whose extra-marital dalliances are splashed across newspaper headlines —Doug and Jackie have been happily married for 12 years. No affairs, no finger-pointing.

Do the ridiculers know that the Christies renew their vows every year on July 8, their wedding anniversary? Or, that they have matching tattoos that declare "Infinite Love"—her on the right arm and him on the left?

Or that Doug actually likes having his wife around? Yes, even on road trips. What? No strip clubs?—a favorite haunt of professional athletes.

— **Scott Soshnick, *Bloomberg News*, N.Y.** (Feb. 07)

Hey Doug and Jackie, thanks for adding us to myspace (http://www.myspace.com/jackieanddouginfinitelove). My fiancée and I are so proud of you two and your relationship. For so long we thought there was no one else out there like us. So much of society promotes infidelity and the player mindset. It takes a real man to lead his woman by example. It takes a strong woman to create the tight, impregnable circle of love in the home. You two are shining examples of both. May God walk with you in your endeavors. I bid you wisdom and strength.

— **G. Jones Harris, author, *Harness the Power Within and Without***

To have and to hold forsaking all others, basketball superstar Doug Christie has made it clear that he's satisfied with the woman at home whom he took as his wife—Jackie Christie. Where commitment is concerned, a Black man's inclination and ability to make that promise of faithfulness to one woman has always been in question. Ironically, when Christie went public with his willingness to do just that, he's been insulted and called every name in the book. What exactly does this say about us?
— **Kate Ferguson,** *Today's Black Woman*

TYRA BANKS SHOW

I just wanted to let you both know that I was watching *The Tyra Show* last night and I respect you so much! Your marriage is an example of what marriage should be about! So many marriages fail, and if we all communicated like you did, and we're all dedicated and devoted like you both are, there would be no cheating, no heartbreak, and no divorces! It's amazing the communication you have. Like I said, I really do respect it, and I wish both of you the most happiness in your lives!
— **Rachael**

I watch your BET show. I JUST LOVE YOU!!!! I'm a married woman, 32 years old, and I've known my husband for 14 years. I love him dearly. I understand how you feel as a wife, and I love the passion you have for your husband and marriage. You represent us women well! You keep being Jackie, no matter what anyone says. Who cares anway? You're only accountable to God, your husband, and your children. You go girl!
— **MM**

I just viewed *The Tyra Banks Show* where you and your husband, Doug, were interviewed by Tyra. I have to say that I fell in love with your relationship and commitment to one another. The father of my son and I just broke up for the first time, and I'm going crazy … I'm in love. Jackie, I know you're a woman of business—you're a wife and a mother—but if you could give me any word of advice I would really appreciate it. I see you and Doug on the TV screen, and it makes me cry, because seeing the two of you is like seeing my man and me, in what I thought would be our future together. Thank you so much!

— Lexi

I watched *The Tyra Show* last night where you and your husband were guests. I just wanted to thank you for your awesome appearance and for allowing the general public inside your hearts. I'm engaged to be married to a professional baseball player and watching you on *The Tyra Show* gave me so much unbelievable strength! … Mrs. Christie, I think it's important that you know how awesome and powerful you are to someone who's also in your shoes! God bless you to the tenth power!

— Martha

I applaud you and your commitment to your husband, his career and none-the-less your business and family. Continue to stand strong! Fight the good fight—LOVE IS WORTH FIGHTING FOR!

— Barbie

No ORDINARY Love

A TRUE STORY OF MARRIAGE AND BASKETBALL!

Doug & Jackie Christie

with MICHAEL LEVIN

Infinite Love Publishing
REDMOND, WA

Published by
Infinite Love Publishing
15127 N.E. 24th Street #341
Redmond, Washington 98052
www.InfiniteLovePublishing.com
888-733-7105

Some names have been changed to protect the privacy of certain individuals.

**Publisher's Cataloging-in-Publication
(Provided by Quality Books, Inc.)**

    Christie, Doug.
       No ordinary love : a true story of marriage and
    basketball! / Doug & Jackie Christie ; with Michael
    Levin.
       p. cm.
    LCCN 2007926543
    ISBN-13: 978-0-9794827-0-0
    ISBN-10: 0-9794827-0-4

       1. Christie, Doug. 2. Christie, Jackie. 3. African
    American basketball players--United States--Family
    relationships. 4. Spouses--United States--Biography.
    5. African American models--United States--Family
    relationships. 6. Marriage.   I. Christie, Jackie.
    II. Levin, Michael Graubart. III. Title.

    GV884.C47A3 2007   796.323'092'2
                        QBI07-600115

Printed in the United States of America

Book Design by Dotti Albertine

God, grant me the SERENITY to
accept the things I cannot change,
COURAGE to change the things I can,
and the WISDOM to know the difference.
Living one day at a time;
enjoying one moment at a time;
accepting hardships as the pathway to peace;
taking, as He did, this sinful world
as it is, not as I would have it:
Trusting that He will make all things right
if I surrender to His Will;
that I may be reasonably happy in this life
and supremely happy with Him
forever in the next.
Amen.

— Reinhold Niebuhr

Thank you!

We want to thank God first and foremost, as He is our
guiding light!

We want to thank our beautiful children for keeping us honest!

We want to thank our parents for all their love and support!

We want to thank our families for helping make us who we are!

We want to thank Ms. Tyra Banks for her inner beauty, friendship,
kindness, and support!

We want to thank Howard, Thea, and Jordan at Fifteen Minutes
Public Relations for getting our message to the world!

We want to thank Scott Soshnick for the inspiration to
keep on going!

We want to thank Mike Tharp for believing in us!

We want to thank Adam Duerson for his incredible kindness.

We want to thank the entire Sacramento Kings organization for
giving us the best years of Doug's career!

We want to thank the fans of Sacramento, in the community, and
all over the world who have been rooting us on all the way!

We want to thank BET for making our reality show a success!

We want to thank the NBA for the platform to showcase Doug's
God-given talent!

We want to thank every NBA team Doug's ever had the
opportunity to play for!

We want to thank you, the reader, for taking the time to learn
our story!

CONTENTS

Invitation

Dear Reader,

We invite you into our world to experience the much talked-about love affair we share. We feel we have some very good tips on love and marriage, and we want you to get to know us better. We invite you to incorporate into your life any and all of the things we do together to keep our love strong and our bond tight.

Doug: As a world-class professional athlete, I will show you how, no matter what the circumstances, I keep my relationship with my wife sacred and how I fall in love with her over and over again.

Jackie: As the wife of an NBA basketball player, a mother of three, and a business woman, I would like to share my experiences with you. I want to offer suggestions on how to keep the fire burning in your own marriage or relationship. I'll share with you how I juggle the demands of motherhood, marriage, and our many businesses ... and still have time to enjoy our beautiful Infinite Love and marriage!

Doug and Jackie Christie

ONE

～

THE ULTIMATUM

Doug: The second most important thing in my life is basketball. The most important thing in my life is my family—my marriage to Jackie; my relationship with our three children—Chantel, Ta'Kari, and Douglas. If you know me, you know how much I love to play the game. It's given us everything we have—a beautiful home, financial security, and the ability to dedicate so much of our time and financial resources to charitable endeavors.

    My pro career has had more twists and turns than I could have imagined, from the time I was initially drafted in the first round by the Seattle SuperSonics—even though a contract dispute made it impossible for me to sign with them. So I was traded to the Lakers, where I got to play alongside Byron Scott, Vlade Divac, James Worthy, and many of the other great players from the Showtime era. From the Lakers I went to New York, and then Toronto, where Isiah Thomas was the general manager of the team and one

1

of the finest people I've ever met. From Toronto, we went to Sacramento, where I played five years on the most amazing team I could imagine. It was just so much fun playing with them. And then I got hurt and was the first to be traded. I went to Orlando, where I played until I realized I needed ankle surgery. My heart ached because I enjoy playing so much and I knew that I would have to rehabilitate it and would be out of the game for a while.

Until this season, my last stop had been with Dallas. In fact, I'll tell you about all of the different stops we've made on the NBA circuit. But after Dallas, it really looked as though I would never get to play again, and I found that devastating. I love the game of basketball, I love playing, and I love competing. It's in my blood. So you can imagine my excitement when the Seattle SuperSonics talked to my agent in September 2006, wanting me to work out for them.

Jackie: We live in Seattle, Washington, so it seemed like our prayers were answered. Doug had been the home-town hero when he played basketball in high school here. We had both grown up in the city as well, and now it would just be a short trip downtown for him to go to work.

Doug: And we wouldn't have to pack!

Well, I went down to the gym to work out with the team, and I wasn't exactly sure of how well I would be able to play. After all, I was coming back from ankle surgery, and you can work out all you want and shoot all the baskets you want at home, but until you actually get on the court with other NBA players, you have no way of gauging how good your game is.

I can tell you this—it was like a dream. I was not just playing better than I thought I could. I honestly believe that while working out with the Sonics, I was playing better than I had in a while. The game just flowed. Sure, it took a day or two for me to find my rhythm, but once I did, it was a great feeling.

On top of that, the players on the team couldn't have been more supportive. Their superstars are Ray Allen and Rashard Lewis, and they seemed delighted to have me on board. I've always been known in the League as a defensive specialist, which means that I free up the shooters from the primary responsibility of sticking guys at the defensive end of the floor. Since I've got that covered, they're free to create, shoot, and put up their numbers. I'm happy because I'm contributing, and the result is winning basketball. Ray Allen and Rashard Lewis had true appreciation for what I was doing, and they told management that they wanted me on their team.

Jackie: Rashard Lewis was even quoted in the newspaper as saying, "It's almost like Doug is a member of the team already."

Doug: Then one day, General Manager Rick Sund approached me in the Sonics' weight room and asked if he, Coach Bob Hill, and I could have dinner. "Sure! Just see my agent! He'll set it up and we can meet." But then it dawned on me; if I'm sitting down in a restaurant with my agent and the coach and maybe Rick Sund, the general manager of the Seattle SuperSonics, word's going to get out really quickly, and maybe that's not the best thing. Deals like this are best done when there's a certain amount of privacy. So instead of a restaurant, I suggested that they come to our home. I'd cook dinner, and we'd sit down and talk.

Jackie: Doug likes to cook. He's very good at it, and a lot of the time he does the cooking for the family. I'll do the laundry and run errands, but the cooking I leave to him.

Doug: It's something I picked up hanging around my grandmother's kitchen, when I was young. I'd just sit there and watch her cook, and sometimes I would ask her how she did this or how she did that. Then I'd start messing around myself. My best friend from childhood, who's still my best friend today, Tyrone Pollard—we call him Tye for short—likes to cook, too. So the two of us will get in the kitchen, turn the music on, and start cooking.

Jackie: I wasn't there. I was told by Doug's agent that it was best if Doug met with them alone, so I went to the gym to work out.

Doug: Tyrone and I cooked up a bunch of food for the Sonics brass—salad, fettuccine, steak with potatoes, vegetables, fine wine—which they passed on, but we had it there for them, just in case. We made sure we had all beverages stocked—anything they might want—from apple juice to lemonade.

The food turned out great. My cooking really took off in college—I was at Pepperdine, which is in Malibu, and I didn't have a lot of money, so I figured if I didn't really learn to cook, I might not eat. Even when I was in Los Angeles and New York, I would still call my grandmother and ask her, "How do you do this?" or "How do you do that?" One time, I cooked a meal for a date with Jackie—it was kind of experimental. I don't remember what it was, but I know I hadn't made it before. So Jackie was my taste-tester.

Jackie: I didn't know that!

Doug: Yeah, it was trial and error. It expanded after she told me, "You cook really good." That encouragement spurred me on to become an even better cook. That's how everything is in our marriage.

Okay, back to dinner with the coach and the general manager of the SuperSonics. We talked basketball for a while. They were inquisitive, asking a lot about the reality show that Jackie and I had been doing. They seemed very uncomfortable about it. If you've heard of us, you might have heard some pretty strange things about us, that we're weird people, that I'm henpecked, that Jackie's controlling, and all sorts of other terrible things that happen not to be true. For some reason, the sports media have been gunning for us practically since we got married. We were surprised at some of the things said about us on the air, even by people with a reputation for responsibility, like Bryant Gumbel. But we partici-pated in the reality show in order for people to see how we really are and that we are not weird.

Jackie: We've gotten so many positive responses from all kinds of people about the show—celebrities, other athletes, and fans. The reaction in e-mails has been unanimous—people are really excited to have an African American couple offered as role models for what a committed marriage can be. That's the most satisfying thing about the show for me—it gave us a chance to show people who we really are, not who the sports media purport us to be.

Doug: Exactly. So I'm staying on a positive keel through this meal—we're having a great talk, everything's looking good, and it just feels as though I'm coming full circle. After all, I was born in Seattle and now it looked like I would have the opportunity to end my career in the Sonics uniform. It just felt right.

That's when the trouble began.

"If we sign you," they asked, "would you have a problem being the thirteenth guy?"

I tried not to let my face show my true feelings, but the question shocked me. Why would they want me to be the thirteenth guy? With no disrespect intended to any of the other members of the Sonics, it was pretty plain to me after a couple of days with the team that I was the third or fourth best player out there. So why would they even hire me if all they wanted me to be was the thirteenth man, who usually never sees the floor unless a player is injured?

"We'll just have to think about that," I said as diplomatically as I could.

They nodded, but I could tell that wasn't the response they were looking for. I wonder what they must have thought of me. Just because I had been injured didn't mean I couldn't play. I had worked incredibly hard to rehab my ankle and I was almost in the best shape of my playing career. Thirteenth man? For a team that had been struggling in the standings for years? I just couldn't figure that one out.

And that's when the real trouble came.

"Look, Doug," they said. "A lot of teams do things their own way when it comes to wives and families of the players. The way we do it is that we sequester the players for training camp. We know obviously that you live here in Seattle, but we'd want you downtown with the players for the whole training camp. *And no visitors allowed.* Would that be a problem?"

It didn't sound very good, but plenty of teams did this. The Lakers under Pat Riley were famous for traveling to Hawaii or Santa Barbara for training camps to focus and let the team bond. So this was an accepted way of doing things in the NBA, although, of course, it wasn't the only way.

Before I could answer, they got to the point they really wanted to make.

"Here's the other thing, Doug," they said. "It's about your wife. Obviously she's a free person and she can do anything she wants, no disrespect intended. But we don't want her traveling to away games. In fact, we don't even want her in the same city where an away game of ours is being played. Is that something you can live with?"

No wives? But if I want to go out and pick up on some girl, it's all good?! No way. I couldn't possibly abide by that! Jackie is my soul mate and my best friend. Jackie always traveled with me, either on the team plane when that was the policy of the team, or she would just fly separately. I took an immediate resentment to this rule.

Jackie: We assumed they had heard all the garbage about us, so it was evident to Doug and me, once he told me what happened, that the rule was aimed at us. Aimed at me.

Doug: I was just shocked. They had obviously bought into

the hype that they had heard about Jackie. I'm not one to use the term "hate" lightly, but I can't imagine what other term would apply when you think about all the abuse, cruelty, and blatant lies that have been hurled her way during our time in the NBA. She's been called names and mocked because of her love for me. Sports reporters seem to take some kind of devilish glee in portraying her as something she isn't. I'll tell you what Jackie is. She's the most loving, supportive, devoted wife I could ever want. She's my soul mate, my best friend, the mother of my children, my business partner, the person I'm destined to spend my life with. Sometimes I say to her, "We'll be together a long time into the future, pushing each other's wheelchairs."

Jackie: How exactly are we supposed to push each other's wheelchairs if we're both in wheelchairs, honey?

Doug: I don't know. Maybe they'll be electric. But the point is that Jackie is portrayed in the media as the exact opposite of who she is. They say that she controls me. They say that she won't let me do interviews with female reporters, which is a lie. They say a million different things about her. And we felt from the direction of the conversation the Sonics management had taken that they must have bought into the falsehoods.

I responded, "Well, I will have to get back to you after I discuss it with my wife."

I'm sure this was also not the response they wanted either, but that's what I said. I was thinking, "This is crazy!" The NBA is fabled for its groupies and so-called hootchies in every city. What most people don't know is that some of those girls aren't just hanging around outside the arena waiting to hook up with one of the players. Sometimes, they're actually on the payrolls of some of the teams—they actually work for some of the teams. I'll get into that later, as well.

But I was sitting there staring at these guys thinking, "Are they out of their damn minds? Women who are keeping the players up all night, out at clubs, in hotel rooms, doing whatever—that's not a distraction to the team? That doesn't affect the way a guy plays? But my bringing my wife along because I want her with me even when I'm on the road—that's a problem somehow? Is this odd or what?"

I wanted them to leave my home before I said something that I would regret.

Jackie: Besides, it's not like they would notice I was there anyway. I'm there for Doug, not them. Mostly, when I travel on the road trips, I hardly see anyone from the team, except at the game or on the team bus or plane, if they allow the family to go.

Doug: It was evident from their facial expressions that they knew that there was no way on earth that I would go along with this business about agreeing not to let my wife travel, or at least be in the same city with me. So they headed out the door, but before they did they were nice enough to say, "Whatever we do, you're always welcome to come to SuperSonics games. If you need tickets, just give us a call."

They then turned to me and said, "Well, if you don't play for us, what are you going to do?" As if they thought that they were my only option, and that since I was not willing to go along with the ultimatum about my wife, I wouldn't have another chance to play. But they were wrong. As I've always said, my wife and my family come first, and basketball, though I love it, does not define me. So I proceeded to tell them that we have other businesses, and that's what I'll be doing. I thanked them for coming and said goodbye.

As I showed them out of our home and closed the door behind them, my heart was sinking. Tickets to a game? I didn't want tickets to a game. I wanted to play for my hometown. I wanted to make the fans of Seattle proud. I knew in my heart I could really help the team, as I've always been a fan and studied their play. But not at the cost of spending time away from my wife. As I said at the outset, the most important thing in my life isn't basketball. It's my family. They come first.

Jackie: Okay, so ... I'm at the gym working out and waiting for my cell phone to ring, so Doug can tell me how great everything went. That his dream was coming true.

Doug: I grabbed the phone to call my wife. I knew Jackie was happy with how things were going—she could tell from the workouts how well I was playing, and how the guys on the team were accepting me, as we usually have these discussions after workouts or games. I had been playing with a lot of pain in Dallas, prior to this moment. Now, I was feeling no pain at all! I'm a trained athlete, so after the third day, my conditioning kicked in, and I was feeling great. I was like, "Oh, honey! We might be playing at home!" But now all my hopes were shattered.

Jackie: So he called me. I said, excitedly, "Honey, tell me how it went!"

Doug: "Nah, I don't think it's gonna work, babe!"

Jackie:	I said to him, "Quit playing with me!" He loves to do things like that—get me going one way when the reality is another way.
Doug:	"It's not gonna work," I said. "I'm serious. Tyrone's sitting here, so I don't want to talk too long right now. Just come on home and I'll give you all the details."
Jackie:	I was like, "Okay, but I don't understand."
Doug:	"When you get home," I told her, "you will."

When she got home, I explained the situation to her. It seemed that they would only accept me on the condition that Jackie not come along on road trips or even be in the same city. Everything was business as usual and everything was okay until they said that she couldn't go on the road.

Jackie:	I couldn't believe it—I thought, "*Wow!* They must have really bought into the untrue stories about me." They didn't even want me in the same city as my own husband.
Doug:	I talked with my agent. It seemed that the team was really concerned about the reality show and about the "closeness" of our relationship, like we were too close for comfort.
Jackie:	We were totally shocked at this point. Our private life is ours, and should not be a concern to anyone.
Doug:	I think someone said I wasn't focused and I didn't want to play anymore.

I think that, just maybe, the whole thing about the reality show was an excuse. They seemed concerned about our close marriage. The show had been filmed over a year before, they weren't filming anymore at the time, and it had only gotten positive responses.

Jackie: My attitude was, if Doug wanted to play with the SuperSonics even under those conditions, it would have been okay with me. I knew how important his dream was to him. And even though I was heartbroken, I would make this sacrifice for my husband.

Doug: There was never any chance of that. Imagine having to guarantee that my wife wouldn't come around. That she would basically be invisible. I mean, where do you get off with something like that?

Jackie: They never even called Doug back directly; they only spoke to his agent after the meeting. They must have known he wouldn't go for it. When Doug told me all of this, I couldn't fathom it! I exclaimed, "They really said *it's me or them?*"

Doug: After I was playing that well it should have been a no-brainer, but instead it was a no-go.

Jackie: It felt like we were all alone and there was no one who could help us. I knew how hard Doug had worked to recover from the surgery and how excited he was to be back on the court. We were envisioning seeing him come to play; he'd be in the green and gold of the Seattle SuperSonics, the team that drafted him. And it would just be a quick drive from home to the arena.

Doug: I wasn't really shocked. I've seen so much in this League that nothing could surprise me. I was trying to stay calm. But they had a problem with me. It hurts because, as a player who takes his craft seriously, I was striving so hard. I really wanted to do this. I was really starting to expand my game and push it harder and harder. To get cut down like that wasn't a good feeling.

Jackie: We've been through so much, especially with the

sports media. Even after he had surgery, some people were saying that he was just pretending to be injured. So to show them he was really hurt, we actually had a press conference and his agent showed the bone spurs that were removed during surgery. We're not the kind of people to make things up. I was really ready to throw in the towel, but it was my husband's career. What really bothered me was that they were calling Doug a quitter in the newspapers. Our kids were seeing this, and they were asking, "Is Dad really a quitter?" And then when the Sonics made that proposition, it hurt.

Doug: I knew Jackie would have supported me if I had made the decision to accept the SuperSonics' offer on their terms and have her not travel, because she loves me. But I would never put anything ahead of my wife.

Jackie: Despite all the stories you hear about me making all his decisions for him, no, I wouldn't be happy about it. But I would stand by my husband.

Doug: My mind was made up even before they had gone out the front door. The only thing that really bothered me was the fact that I wouldn't get to play with my hometown team. That was the thing that I had the hardest time with. I just figured, well, it wasn't meant to be, and there would be another opportunity down the road. There's still twenty-nine other teams in the NBA, and at least one of them might think that I could help them and not be concerned with my closeness to my wife!

TWO

~

THE FOUNDATION

Jackie: I was the third youngest of nine kids. My dad wasn't in the household, but I knew him well, and I had a stepfather. For many years, though, my mom was the sole caregiver. I learned so much from her about how to raise a family and even how to run a business—there's nothing easy about running a large family like we had. In some ways, I don't know how she did it, and I marvel at her ability to keep everything together.

I'm a big list person—I love to make lists of everything that I need to do, not just for the next day or the following week, but even for the next year. Not just things to check off the list but also goals—things I want to achieve and family goals, too. Then, as I'm able to check those things off, especially the big ones, it gives me a very good feeling of accomplishment. Not to mention I have more time to do other things that I want to do. I definitely learned my organizing skills from my mom, there's no doubt about that.

We didn't have a lot of money, but we were a very close-knit family. My mom's love was truly infinite for all of us kids. I saw that each of us meant the same to her, and we all meant the world to her. And even though we didn't have a lot of "things," I learned a very important lesson from her—if you have family, you have it all.

Our cars wouldn't always be new, but they would be neat. Even if the radiator was steaming, my mom would find a way to get it fixed and we'd be on our way. She taught me the importance of making the best of whatever I had.

Fashion was the biggest thing in my life, even when I was three or four years old. I knew back then I was destined to grow up and be a model or an actress and wear fancy clothes. That was the vision I had for myself. I would do fashion shows with all my siblings. I would tell my sisters and brothers, "Okay, now it's your turn to sing a song." At first, they were annoyed when they didn't do well, but then it became a family tradition, and everybody loved it. My mom would make clothing for us, and you could say that was the start of my fashion career. I always had the support of my family, no matter what I wanted to do.

By the time I was ten or eleven years old, I was already modeling in shows at the local mall or various city events. Of course I never told my mother, but I was actually embarrassed by our family car. I would always tell my family to come twenty minutes late. If the show was starting at ten, I would tell them to get there at 10:20, so that no one could see our car—since they'd be inside already—eight kids of all different sizes spilling out, the car sputtering, my mom's big hair. She had so much hair! I laugh now that I was so embarrassed then. Okay, I wasn't actually embarrassed, but I just didn't want people to see this. All the other girls with whom I modeled came from families with nice cars. I just felt we didn't have the right transportation, I guess.

Our family was close, but I still sometimes fought with my sisters a lot because, well, you know, the whole sibling rivalry thing. But they knew me to be a kindhearted person who forgave easily, so they would find it in their hearts to forgive me.

My mother always arranged it so that a bunch of us could attend the same school at the same time. Typically, there would be five of us from our family attending the same school. People knew that if you messed with one of us, you had to deal with all of us. Through it all, I had the attitude that I would be an actress or a model, and I didn't tell too many people that, because I didn't want to get teased about it. But even through elementary school, we were still putting on those shows, and sometimes we'd charge money—say, two dollars—so we could raise money to make more costumes. Aside from that, I was just a typical kid. I loved to go outside, play hopscotch, read my mom's fashion magazines, and go to the local stores and just see what they had—window-shop, I guess.

At Christmastime, we would sign up for different programs that supported big, single-parent families like ours. These are programs like Toys for Tots. You could request three items and write them down on a list, and more fortunate people would get the lists from the charities and buy the toys, and donate them to the organization. That way, you pretty much always knew what you were getting. I always wanted Barbie dolls and fashion items. If Mom made enough money, she'd buy us presents, too. But the main thing we got from her was love.

Today, people see us on the reality show living in a beautiful mansion in an upscale neighborhood, but I was born a long way from the proverbial white picket fence. I knew growing up that I wanted to save enough money to take care of myself and my family and help other people out, but more than that, I wanted the beautiful relationship with a soul mate that unfortunately eluded my mom and so many other women, and men for that matter. I knew that my soul mate was out there for me, and I was completely dedicated to finding him. I knew that expression—"instead of looking for the right person, be the right person." So I tried to be everything I wanted him to be—loving, kind, and good-hearted. And I prayed a lot. In my quest for this person, my mom ended up calling me "the Blazer," because the moment in a relationship I knew it was wrong, it was over. I knew I'd find my Prince Charming. When I met Doug, I got what I always dreamed of.

I'm a little ahead of myself. Back in high school, I was modeling and doing gymnastics. I was pretty good at gymnastics until a freak accident—a mirror sliced my left Achilles tendon. I needed surgery and I was in a cast for half of ninth grade. It wasn't too bad because I was popular in high school and all the boys saw my temporary disability as a way to flirt and so they helped me out a lot. As soon as the doctors took the cast off, I tried to come back too soon. I ran too hard, and it ruptured again. That was the end of my gymnastics career.

Girls can be really tough on each other, especially in high school. Some of the girls then were jealous of me and they would try to pick on me. They would say things like, "She thinks she's cute." They would throw these little jealousy fits. I might have been cute, but I was tough, too! In high school, I quickly developed a reputation—you'd better not mess with me, because I've got lots of sisters and brothers, and I'll fight you all by myself if I have to.

One of the best things that ever happened to me was being in a girls dance group. I can't recall the group's name, but we performed at the Bubbling Brown Sugar event at the local high schools' basketball games. I loved ensemble dancing because of the bonding among the girls. We had something special that we could do and we could perform. It was fun because despite the fact that I came from such a big family, I was always something of a loner, always just thinking about growing up and becoming a model. Once I was in that group, there was really no stopping me. No one in my family believed I could dance! But I brought my mom down to see the show one time, and she was so impressed.

After high school, I continued to study, to improve myself, to develop, and find my path. I attended community college for two years. Whatever interested me, I would study. I went to bank teller school and got my certificate. I studied computers, worked at a cleaner's, worked in different department stores, whatever it took, to keep progressing forward. All the while still modeling and loving every minute of it. I was popular, in part, I think, because I knew a lot about fashion. Everybody loves clothing, and girls love to talk about clothing, so I always had friends who shared that interest with me. I pretty much liked to relax instead of party, so I wasn't in the kind of crowd that was out every night. I was looking for something, and I knew that it would find me. Settling down was my number one priority. After that, my next priority was helping people in life. Even then I knew that I wanted to help as many people as I could. As a child, I was branded as soft because I would give everything away, but I just loved people and I wanted to help them.

I had boyfriends, but I had never had a friend who was a boy until I met Joey B. That was different, just to have a male figure in my life who was a friend and not a potential romantic interest. And one day Joey B. said, "I have someone for you to meet. I think you'll really like him." Of course, it was Doug, and I thank Joey B. to this day.

You could say I had a fun childhood with lots of playmates, unlike Doug, who got spoiled being an only child.

Doug: This is your turn! Leave me out of it!

Jackie: Okay! So we moved down to south Seattle. There was a store called Busy Bee Greens and Things. Doug's mom was part owner. I didn't know the Christies back then. I just knew that she had the best candy in town. My mom would treat us on special occasions with candy from their store. We were always like, "Let's go down to the store. They've got all the latest candies!" I never realized that Doug was one of the kids playing video games in the back at his mother's store. He knew one of my little sisters. He would later remember seeing her around. But somehow, our paths didn't cross back then. You could say we lived parallel lives until Joey B. introduced us. It was ironic. We lived in the same neighborhoods, and we were the same type of kids. We came from the same type of background, and yet somehow we never knew each other.

Doug: Life's all about timing. We weren't supposed to meet then. We were supposed to meet when we did.

Jackie: That's right. Okay, your turn.

Doug: Okay. Here goes. My father was black and my mother was white, and she was very young when I was born. They took me and warded me to the state. My grandfather, Dale Christie, came and got me, vouched for my mother, and brought me back to her.

I was an only child, so my whole childhood was basically my mom and me, and of course, all my friends. We first lived in Bellevue with my grandfather, who was a part owner in a skating rink, so I would stay at the rink a lot because I could skate there all the time. I'd also sleep in the back of the rink, get up, skate, go back to bed. It was great. Then my mom and I moved to the south end of Seattle. It was a lower income area, and she was one of the few white people in the neighborhood. Race was never an issue with me. I never looked at color lines that way. I didn't care about that. Around this time, my mom worked at a local grocery store. Everybody knew my mom. Wherever I went, it was, "Oh, you're Norma's son!" As I grew up, and people recognized me for basketball, it shifted—then they would say to her, "Oh, you're Doug's mom!"

Neither work nor school was a passion for me when I was a kid. Instead, not surprisingly, it was sports. Soccer was my first love. I played the game from the age of seven until about ten. I was pretty good, too, playing left wing and right wing. Then I met my mother's boyfriend, who was a basketball player. And that's when I really fell in love with the game. Practically from the first moment I touched the ball I knew—*this is what I like, and this is what I'm going to play.* School didn't interest me very much at all, but basketball sure did.

My father lived ninety minutes south of Seattle in a town called Longview, Washington. I met him for the first time when I was about six years old. I got to go down and hang out with him. For a city kid like me, Longview was really different—it was more like the country. Up in Seattle, I lived in a predominantly black neighborhood. Longview was almost totally white. There were only two black families in the whole town. It was a great education for me as a young person to see both sides of the fence. At the time, Longview represented the wilderness—my dad and I would go fishing and hunting there, and I just loved it. "Man," I would say to myself, "this is awesome!" That would be during the summer. During the school year, however, I'd be in Seattle with my mom.

I got into recreational league junior basketball in Seattle, and in my second year, our team won a championship. That was the coolest thing ever, and I realized that although I might not have put it in those words at the time, succeeding in sports helped me to get over the insecurities I had developed growing up without a father in my home. I lived in a rough neighborhood, and I didn't have brothers or sisters. It was just me, by myself. Other guys had their dads or older brothers to give them confidence. I found confidence in athletics. And since everyone in the neighborhood knew my mom, I didn't run into a lot of problems with the other kids.

I feel as though I've had an angel watching out for me from my earliest childhood. Some of my friends were even murdered. They were some of my best friends when I was younger, and we grew apart as we took different paths in life. Luckily, I never got involved with some of the dangerous activities that they discovered. I made the choice to go in the other direction.

That's why being a father is so important to me— I know there are certain things that our children will never have to go through, certain temptations that will never befall them, simply because I'm here for them.

My mom was always my biggest advocate and my strength. For so many years, she served both as my mother and my father. I hope you enjoyed those Father's Day cards, Mom! Wanting to do things for her became my driving force. I wanted to buy her a house when I grew up. I wanted to give her financial security. Our relationship spurred me to keep on pushing to succeed as an athlete, and I dedicated my life to basketball. Skipping school wasn't an option for me, because my mom would take a seat with my best friend Tyrone's mom at all the games. She knew what was going on, and the school was right across the street from her job.

After I started to have some success in basketball, I found it was addictive. I really enjoyed the game. That's what I wanted to do—play all the time. By sixth grade, however, my grades weren't good. I was just playing basketball and hanging out with my friends. My mom told me that if I didn't get it together, she'd send me to live with my dad. I didn't think she'd do it ... but she did! So off I went to Longview.

While I lived with my father I excelled in athletics. My father made sure that I was getting good enough grades to play ball. If I didn't get good grades—he made it clear—no sports, no fishing, no hunting. So I got my act together in that way.

I went back to Seattle for eighth grade, and Longview for ninth grade and part of tenth before finally deciding to stay with my mom and finish high school in Seattle. My mom enrolled me in Rainier Beach High School, in our neighborhood, and through a friend of hers she also set up a workout for me with the basketball coaches. After seeing me play, they said, "We've got a place on the team for you." Suddenly, I found myself on the varsity team of the very best high school in the state—a true blessing. The following year, basketball suddenly took off to a completely different stratosphere for me. I was All-Metro my junior year and Senior Player of the Year, with our team winning its first state championship in basketball.

I graduated high school that year, having made some great achievements in track as well. I jumped seven feet in the high jump, which won first in the state. Things were looking up for me! The downside was my grades. I had good enough grades to get by and to be noticed by colleges. But there's just this little thing called the SAT. If you don't score at least seven hundred on your SAT, the NCAA says you're not eligible to play during your freshman year of college (better known as Prop 48). This certainly limited my options.

Since I was growing up in Seattle, my thoughts naturally turned to the University of Washington, but that didn't work out. Instead, I got an invitation from Pepperdine, down in Malibu, so I decided to visit. Naturally, I fell in love with the campus—who wouldn't, with its incredible views of the Pacific right in the heart of Malibu? I also knew it was time for me to get away from home and stand on my own. I felt I had to test myself in a totally different environment.

Pepperdine couldn't have been better to me. They told me that whether I got the minimum score necessary on the SAT to play my first year or not, they would still honor my scholarship. I'm a loyal kind of person and I respect loyalty, so I told them, "You've got yourself a ballplayer." At the time, Jim Harrick was the coach, and he was headed to UCLA, but I stayed at Pepperdine because the assistant coach who recruited me, Tom Asbury, would be replacing him. I'll say this—going to Pepperdine was one of the hardest transitions I've ever been through. Educationally, standards were a lot higher, and being around a bunch of well-to-do college students proved to be interesting. I couldn't play basketball because of Prop 48, the rule about the SAT I mentioned, so instead I played intramural basketball. I wasn't even allowed to watch the team practice. I was homesick and by Christmas break, I was distraught. I went into the coach's office extremely upset and saying that I wasn't coming back.

He asked me if I was sure, and I said, "Yeah, I'm sure."

Coach was very thoughtful. He responded, "Well, everything's waiting here for you if you change your mind."

I packed everything I owned into the trunk I had brought with me, and I headed back home. And I'll tell you what, that trip back to Seattle during Christmas of freshman year was the best thing that ever happened to me. When I returned to the old neighborhood, I found everybody was doing exactly the same routine, and I wasn't missing out on anything.

During that Christmas break, I made up my mind that I was going to return to Pepperdine. This was a big turning point in my life. I knew it would be difficult, but I also knew I was up for the challenge. I couldn't be around the team, so I hit the books. That way, I was going to be eligible to play the next year.

So after making it through my freshman year, I came back my sophomore year. But junior year was when everything kind of exploded. All of a sudden they were lining up tables for NBA scouts at our games. I'd go out and shoot before the game and I'd see the sports administrator from Pepperdine, Mike Zapolski, laying out credentials from the Lakers, the Bulls, as well as other teams. I'd say to him, "Who are they coming to see?"

"You," he'd say.

Well, my mind started going crazy. I thought, "I could leave college early and go into the NBA." Instead, I hurt my knee at the end of the year. I was Player of the Year my junior year at Pepperdine.

However, that knee injury was kind of a message to me—stay there. So I stayed and played my senior year, and then I was drafted in the first round, by Seattle. It looked like I was going home. And around that same time, I met Jackie.

Jackie: When I met him, I thought—

Doug: *Hot guy!*

Jackie: That's not what I thought! Okay, that's not the only thing I thought. He seemed like a nice person, and we could go on from there.

Doug: And we did. So, that's where we came from. That's how we started off.

～

THREE

MY PRINCE CHARMING

Jackie: It wasn't an easy road, from the time we met until the time we were both ready for a commitment. But that's why you should never give up hope. Infinite love can require infinite patience, especially at the start.

Doug: You've got to remember that I'm coming from a background where in some ways womanizing was considered normal. I really didn't know, or understand for that matter, what it took for a committed relationship to work. I always knew what I wanted—I wanted what we have now. But I didn't have any way of knowing how to get there. So I was cautious. I took my time.

Jackie: As I stated earlier, we had a mutual friend, Joey B. He told each of us, "I have the perfect person for you to meet." So he put it together—we would meet at a restaurant/sports bar in Seattle.

Doug: It was called Jersey's.

Jackie: When I first saw Doug, he was standing in the middle of the room, and there were a lot of ladies standing around him. I thought, "Uh-oh! Maybe he has a girl-friend, or girlfriends!"

Doug: Once I saw *her,* I said to myself, "She's beautiful!" But I played it cool. I just said, "Pleasure to meet you." We all had a good time talking and whatnot, but nothing was too serious. When Joey B. called me a few days later, I was with my buddy Tyrone. Joey wanted to know if I wanted to see Jackie again since they were good friends. I was like, "Heck yeah, that would be cool!" So we got together again at her place—Tye, Joey B., and I. She had a nice condo in downtown Seattle overlooking the water. We all had a great time talking, watching music videos, laughing, and just relaxing. It felt right. Occasionally, our eyes would lock and we would share a brief moment as if she and I were the only two people in the room. When it was time to go, she walked us downstairs to our cars, and the whole time I wondered how to ask her for her number. But I didn't have to—she asked me if I wanted it!

Jackie: No, I didn't! I didn't do that! I would never do that! He asked if I would give it to him. So I did, but not before Joey B. shot me a dirty look and said, "Oh no, you didn't." Of course, I thought he was joking because he was smiling, but Joey really was saying no. It was awkward for a moment because Joey B. and I were good friends and so were Doug and he, but Doug was just so sweet, so I gave him my number. They drove off and I went back up to my condo and called it a night.

Doug didn't call for a while and I all but forgot about him until I started to see him around town, at comedy events, and restaurants, but I would just ignore him. I thought he was just joking around. I didn't think he was serious about me at all.

Doug: Gotta know how to reel 'em in.

Jackie: So, one night my girlfriends invited me out to a club called Celebrities. I much preferred to stay home in bed reading or watching my favorite show, but I thought, "What the heck, why not?" As soon as we entered the club, I immediately saw Doug. I was completely caught off guard, but gave him a smile. He smiled back and I began to shake my head at him as I thought, "Mm, mm, mm, you are a true player." But he rushed over and grabbed my hand and pulled me to the dance floor. The way he moved was mesmerizing. He looked good. I thought thoughts I knew I couldn't tell my mother. He kept his gaze steadily affixed with mine, and it was so intense I thought I might pass out. I knew I wanted to know him better but there was one small problem that led to a little incident later that night.

You see, I wasn't exactly single. I was, but newly single, and the logistics had not been discussed in enough detail with my ex, I guess, whom I had dated for a little while. We were now just friends and he didn't have any official ties to me. He felt differently and began to make a scene. He approached me, yelling my name, saying things like, "What are you doing, Jackie? You're mine. You're my girl."

Of course, Doug saw all this and I was worried that now he wouldn't call. I attempted to calm the other gentleman down and told him I would call him the next day to clarify things. He accepted it and went away. Doug didn't seem to be bothered by it and he promised to call me that same night. He asked if I was okay. I said yes, and he smiled and said good night.

My girlfriends and I left the club and returned to my place. We planned to watch videos and eat popcorn—my favorite. Also, they were going to stay the night. I was just getting out of the shower and then the phone rang. I was perturbed, to say the least—it was two a.m. The phone rang three times and the caller hung up. I put on my pajamas and went out to the living room to join my friends, who had made sleeping arrangements on the floor. The phone rang again. This time, I picked up.

"May I speak to Jackie?" a male voice asked.

"Speaking," I replied.

"How are you?" he asked.

Well, since this was the first time I had ever heard this voice over the phone, I was not sure I knew who it was. Also, I had an unlisted number, so it must be someone I knew, I thought.

"Do you know who this is?" the voice asked.

"Not really," I responded, trying to play it cool.

"We danced tonight," he told me.

Before I could say anything, he added, "And your boyfriend got mad."

Well, needless to say, my heart dropped. I knew at that moment it was who I wanted it to be. I never noticed that my girlfriends had turned down the volume on the TV to eavesdrop. Their faces said it all when they heard me call his name.

They squirmed and giggled loudly, so I got up from the couch and went into my room, my sanctuary. I lay down on my bed so I could be more comfortable to talk to him. The view of the water from my room was amazing and added just the right touch to our late-night conversation. Doug was at his apartment with his friend Tye and his sister Monica. They were cooking breakfast ... at two a.m. I thought, "My kind of guy!" He said he wanted to keep his promise and call me, and also just to hear my voice. I about lost it. This man was arousing feelings in me that I thought couldn't be. I longed to look into his eyes again right then, but I knew it was impossible. So we talked a little while longer and said goodbye for the second time in one night. We exchanged promises to speak the following day. It seemed like forever until we spoke again.

When he finally called the next day, he invited me to dinner that same night. He took me to a good restaurant in Seattle called Ralph's. It turned out that he was a really nice guy, not like a lot of athletes are supposed to be. You hear things about how athletes just kind of go through women and do not take them seriously, or do not take anything seriously. Doug was the opposite of that. He was very thoughtful, soft-spoken, well-mannered, interested in me, interested in life. It just felt great from the start.

Doug: I took her to a neighborhood in Seattle very close to where we live right now. We went for a long walk and we talked about what we wanted in life.

Jackie: We were inseparable after that first date. Doug had been drafted, but he wasn't playing in the NBA just yet.

Doug: We knew immediately that we would be together. We were spending quite a bit of time together, except when I had stuff to do related to basketball. We were

	always hanging out, going to movies, concerts, or whatever.
Jackie:	I realized that he liked the same things I did. Neither of us were big club-goers—we weren't into noisy scenes. We really had a lot in common. It's amazing—now we've been together fifteen years. That's a lot of time!

Doug became a very special person to me very quickly. I looked forward to his phone calls. He'd call and say something like, "I'm hungry. I want to go for a ride. Do you want to go with me?" We'd eat, or we'd go up to Queen Anne, an observation point, and look out at the view of our beautiful city. Doug was always laid back and romantic, never pushy. He was relaxed and fun to be around.

Doug:	You thought so, huh?
Jackie:	Yes, babe. At the time, I didn't even know he could play basketball that well. I knew he was a basketball player. Take one look at him and you can see he's an athlete. But I had no idea just how good he was. I'll say this—thanks to him, I fell in love with the game.

By this time Doug and I had been dating for a long while, and it was our 6-month anniversary. Doug had to go out of town to see his old coach at Pepperdine for a week, and I was not feeling well at all. So I had to cancel two modeling jobs I had been booked for and decided to go to the doctor, because my stomach was now nauseous and I had breast tenderness. Deep down, I knew that those were signs of impending motherhood. I was sooo scared! I told no one I was going, but I knew I had to, since even the smell of food made it worse. So when the doctor came in after my exam with the words, "I have good news for you, dear—you're not sick with a stomach virus, you're pregnant," I about cried. I looked into her eyes and said, "Excuse me, could you repeat that?" as I tried to clear my head. My heart was beating so fast and hard, and I felt scared but happy, excited yet confused.

I needed to get out of there as fast as I could, and as soon as I was outside, I was then free to scream. I believe I did, but then I laughed hysterically, because I had a sense of immediate calm, knowing I wasn't sick. The thought that there was a little human being growing inside of me, and the man I loved was responsible for it being there, made me giddy. I didn't know what to do.

I wanted to just walk and think and walk some more, and before I knew it I was home at my place, riding the elevator up. I was in a fog of sorts as I entered my condo. My life as I knew it would be changed forever by what I had just learned, and I knew I had to talk to Doug. I had to share with him the good news—we were going to be parents together. We were going to raise our baby ... or so I thought!

For the coming days, I walked around in sheer happiness, knowing those sweet nights we shared had produced a gift so special, meant only for the two of us. Doug couldn't get home fast enough. I spoke to him on the phone a couple of times before he arrived back in Seattle, but this was news to share in person. The phone would not do. I got up the morning he was due home, dressed in his favorite colors for me so I would look my best, and went to the airport to pick him up. His hug was so warm and soulful, and

I couldn't wait to share my news. We talked and laughed, and stopped at his mother's job on the way to my place as he said he missed me so and wanted to make up for lost time. I knew what that meant, but first I had to talk to him and look into his eyes to feel his response to our news.

As soon as we got up to my place, he hugged me again and we kissed—a deep, passionate kiss—and then I asked if he was hungry. He said, "Yes, but first, what's this news you mentioned on the phone the other night you had for me?" Of course, I wasn't really myself, so I had forgotten I said it but figured now was as good a time as any, so out with it I came. And he just looked at me with those gorgeous hazel eyes of his, and his smile faded, to be replaced by a serious expression. He said, "Are you sure?" and I said yes, suddenly sensing that maybe it wasn't good news after all. But then he said, "Wow, this is some big news. I hope you don't mind if I go for a walk alone for a bit because I need to think. This is big, babe."

Choking back my tears and trying to stay calm, I said, "Sure, whatever you need. Hey, maybe we can just talk tomorrow."

And he said, "Are you sure?" I said yes, and he kissed my forehead and left. Well, I was devastated at that point. I was scared and confused by his reaction, but knew through it all that the little person in my tummy would be loved no matter what. I had made up my mind—it is ours, and I will be there for our child. I said a prayer and went to bed. I didn't hear from Doug for two days, and by then I had shared the news with my closest friend, Shelly. She told me to give him time, he would call.

I was preparing some tea and drawing a bath when the phone rang. It startled me. I turned to answer and realized it might be someone I did not feel like talking to, but I answered anyway, and it was Doug. He said, "Hello, beautiful, how do you feel?" I said, "Okay, I guess, how about you?" And he said, "I will feel much better if you say you'll forgive me for the other night." I said, "Why, you only asked for time to work out your thoughts."

Doug said, "Yes, but I should have told you that I was scared. I was surprised and not sure what to do. But now I've thought it through, and I'm a lucky man, babe, and my child, *our* child, is blessed to have you for a mommy! Thank you for my little person, Jackie. We will make great parents, and we have a lot of planning to do, so are you going to invite me over or not so we can get started?"

Through my tears of joy, I was able to say, "Absolutely, I am."

Doug: Around this time, Seattle traded Benoit Benjamin and me to the Los Angeles Lakers for Sam Perkins, when the news came from my agent that I was about to become a Laker. I was overjoyed. I went to L.A. and we held a press conference to make the official announcement. Magic Johnson was there and I was in awe, since I had watched and emulated him since I was a kid—and now I would play on a team that he had helped make so great.

To say the least, it was a lot for me to take in. I immediately found a place in Marina del Rey because I loved looking out at the water. With only forty games or so left in my rookie season, I was truly learning. I played my first game in Philadelphia, and it was memorable for one reason only. I walked into the locker room to grab my jersey and as I picked it up I noticed that my name was misspelled. It read C-H-R-I-S-I-T-E! I smiled and thought, "This isn't the way to start out," but I chose to remain optimistic and I played sparingly, but well.

Jackie remained living in Seattle, and she would come down to L.A. to visit me often. During this time, she was carrying our child and needed to remain near her doctor. When the time approached for Jackie to give birth, my anticipation and nerves were elevated. I was so excited to meet our new arrival. We had found out by this time that the baby was a girl. I always knew I wanted a daughter, and now Jackie was giving me one. I was ecstatic, to say the least.

Before I knew it, the season was over. We took Phoenix and the great Charles Barkley to a final game 5 in the first round of the playoffs, but we couldn't pull it off. L.A. was great. I was going to be in the starting lineup on a good, young team with some great veterans like James Worthy and Byron Scott. During training camp, I was in great shape and playing well. At our first pre-season game, against the Utah Jazz, I came down and sprained my ankle and was out for a while. When I returned to the court I was playing great.

Jackie: After Chantel was born, I moved to Los Angeles. I got my own apartment in Marina del Rey, close to where Doug was living. He was sharing an apartment with a few buddies, living the single man's lifestyle of the NBA. I wanted him to slow down and be a complete family with us, but he wasn't ready. I felt at times he would never be ready, and it was extremely hard to deal with that assumption. But we were close by each other nonetheless, and we were raising our daughter together.

Also, my mother had moved down to help me with the baby, so I could continue to work.

Doug: I was hanging out with buddies, being twenty-two in the NBA, just having a good time. No focus, young and dumb, as I like to say.

Jackie: He wanted the best of both worlds—he wanted me, and he also wanted to hang out with his friends. I was working at the time, and was waiting to see how things would work out with Doug and me. I knew that he was my soul mate and I knew that he would be in my life, for the rest of my life, in one shape or form. After all, we already had a child together. I was hoping that it would be in terms of marriage, but I knew it may not happen. I tried to make the best of the situation anyway.

Doug: I knew that I had been wearing things thin between us. I truly only felt happy and content when we were together. Inside, I knew it was time for a change, even though it still took a while.

Jackie: The longest "while" of my life!

Anyway, one day he called to say that he'd been thinking a lot about us, and that if I wanted to have a real relationship, he'd like that, too. He told me that he would move the guys out of his apartment and that the baby and I would move in with him. I was elated, because for eight months I would attend the Laker games on my own with Chantel, to support Doug. That was the hardest part—after the game, he would go out with his friends, and the baby and I would just go home.

So when he asked me to move in, at first I played it cool a little bit. I teased him—I said I needed some time to think about it, as I had my career to consider. Then I saw the disappointment in his eyes, and I told him I was just joking and I would love to move in with him and be a family. So we did, shortly after that.

Once the summer came, we headed back to Seattle, as Doug had bought a house there recently. We were just getting settled in when suddenly bad news struck. Doug found out that he had to get ankle surgery.

Doug: I wasn't happy about needing surgery at such a young age, but this was the career I chose. After surgery I started rehab, and training camp was approaching fast. Right about that time was the NBA Draft. I should have seen the writing on the wall when the Lakers drafted Eddie Jones, a guard out of Temple University. I was still optimistic about returning and thought I would be fine. So I headed off to training camp in Hawaii.

Not being able to play or defend my spot on the team was tough. I felt powerless just sitting there watching the guys go ahead without me. Then Jerry West called me in my room and asked if I would come up to his suite. On the way up in the elevator, I was thinking, "What could this be about?"

I knocked on the door and he answered. We exchanged pleasantries and then he cut right to the point.

"We're going to trade you or one of the other

guards on the team," he said. "You can go to either the Clippers or the Knicks."

I thought to myself, "Hold your face—don't let him see the pain of rejection." I'm sure he could, though. At the same time, this was business, so I got it together. The Knicks had just been to the Finals the year before and New York was as far away from L.A. as I could get. So I calmly replied, "Please send me to New York." I shook his hand and thanked him for my time in L.A., and I headed back to my room to pack.

Jackie: When I heard the news that he was traded to the Knicks, I thought, "What are we"—meaning the baby and I—"going to do?"

Doug: Since I had bought the home in Seattle, we decided Jackie and our baby would still live in it. Back then, the neighborhood wasn't developed all the way. They were scared to be out there. Most of the time, Jackie wouldn't even stay in the house.

Jackie: I'd stay at my mom's. Then I got an apartment downtown for a while. Doug went to New York to play for the Knicks, and he started to live the fast life again, only this time would be his last. I had had enough, and I made my decision to just live my life and take care of our baby. I loved Doug with all my heart, but it seemed he was still not ready to settle down. And then one day he called to say, "Come to New York for a month." So after thinking it over, I headed to New York with Chantel.

Doug: New York was a much more difficult experience than I had imagined, and I found myself missing Jackie and Chantel even more than I thought I would. When I arrived in the city, training camp was just ending.

On the first day I went to see Coach Pat Riley. I was a little nervous. Here was a man who's an icon in the NBA. I really didn't know what to expect, so I just listened.

He said to me, "Doug, I'm going to be honest with you, you aren't going to play for me." I inhaled deeply. He continued, "I already have my team, my guys that I went through training camp with. So, my advice to you is to work on your game. Take this time to improve."

"Thank you, Coach," I replied.

And that was about it. As I headed out the door I thought, "I don't even get a chance." But then I said to myself, "I can respect his honesty," and I vowed to work my butt off. And I did.

Jackie: During our visit, we had a wonderful time and re-established our bond. Doug began to change and began to ask me more serious questions, like, "Could I live with him forever," and so on. By the time Chantel and I left to return to Seattle, I had more reason to hope that it was a new beginning.

Doug: I learned quite a bit that year about hard work. Coach Riley pushed us to the limit. The team was great. Charles Oakley, Patrick Ewing, John Starks, Herb Williams, Anthony Mason, and Derek Harper—who taught me a lot about defense. I was closest to Charles Oakley from day one. "Oak" took good care of me. He was a great friend and even better teammate.

The fans in New York were some of the best in the NBA. Herb Williams would school me on all of the nuances of the NBA game. That's why, still to this day, I try to pass on that knowledge to the rookies or younger guys whom I encounter. Those games in Madison Square Garden were really special. From Reggie Miller scoring nine points in about six seconds in the playoffs, to Michael Jordan scoring fifty-five—I took it all in. We didn't win the championship, but the education was well worth it. Jackie and Chantel would come often and we would have great times. Christmas, Thanksgiving—we never missed holidays.

Jackie: Slowly but surely, we were becoming a true family. But it would take a few more life experiences before we were ready to take that next step.

FOUR

~

O, CANADA!

Doug: After my first year playing for the Knicks, Pat Riley resigned and they hired Don Nelson. I was sorry to see Pat go, but I was optimistic that maybe I would get some playing time with the new coach. It turns out that that was not to be. One day while Jackie was visiting me at my home, the doorbell rang. It was the Knicks' trainer and some others from the organization. The trainer said, "Doug, I brought some news. You've been traded to Toronto."

    I thanked him and after he left I turned and looked at Jackie like, "Toronto?" It was their inaugural season and I didn't know anything about them except that Damon Stoudamire was the point guard, and Isiah Thomas was the general manager. Jackie said that she could handle the packing and told me not to worry. So off to Toronto I went.

Jackie: The way they arrived, it looked like the military reporting bad news. From Doug's point of view, though, it was very good news. He was out of a

45

tough situation where he wasn't able to contribute and was going to Toronto, so this was a big step forward in Doug's career.

Doug: When I arrived in Toronto I met with Isiah, and he said, "I know what you've been through. I just want you to play as hard as you can. If you mess up, it's okay. We just want you to have the freedom to get comfortable, first and foremost."

I was thinking, "Whoa! Now this is a novel idea!" I very quickly went from not playing in New York to playing more than forty minutes a night in Toronto.

Jackie: I visited Doug in Toronto a couple of times. I thought, "Nice place. Cold but nice."

When the season ended, Doug came home to Seattle. We were out one day having lunch and we saw an older couple, and we started talking about life. And Doug had an epiphany. He saw everything clearly. He said these magic words: "Baby, I'm sorry it's taken me so long. You see, I knew where I wanted to go, but I just didn't know how to get there."

I said, looking into his eyes, "What are you saying, honey?"

Doug: I put my finger gently on her mouth, to quiet her, so I could tell her what I needed to say.

Jackie: My heart was beating so fast I didn't know if I could stand it.

Doug: I knew at that moment that I wanted to spend the rest of my life with her, and I wanted her to know she was my queen.

Jackie: His eyes welled with tears and I wondered if it was just another goodbye. But he went on to say that he loved me and he was sorry for any pain he had ever caused me. By now, I also had tears in my eyes. It had been so long and at times I thought I would never hear what he had to say next.

Doug: I asked her to be my wife, to be my soul mate and best friend.

Jackie: I couldn't believe my ears, and I started to cry and laugh at the same time, something I've done my whole life whenever I'm nervous.

Doug: She even asked me if I was joking. "Hell, no!" I told her. Then I asked her, "Will you marry me and be mine forever?"

Jackie: Of course, I said yes. We immediately began to make plans, because there was no reason to wait.

Doug: And just three days later, we got married. Jackie was nervous all the way to the "I do's." As we were preparing to walk down the stairs, she looked at me and said, "Doug, are you positive about this? You can change your mind! We can tell everyone we changed our minds and still eat the cake." I looked at her and said, "Girl, come on down these stairs so I can make you my wife!"

Jackie: We got married, and he's been upstanding in every way. It's a fairy tale, but it wasn't easy. We went through a lot.

Doug: By that point, I had really begun to feel the emptiness of the life I was leading, without Jackie by my side. The life of the single guy in the NBA had lost its appeal; you could put it that way.

Jackie: He knew he didn't want that anymore. A man has to be ready for a relationship—not forced or coaxed or convinced. And he finally became ready, in his own way, in his own time.

Doug: When you know it, you know it in your soul. You

can't put it into words. It's hard to explain, so I don't try to make people understand. I take my marriage seriously. It's not a joke or a game or a fly-by-night thing. THIS IS MY FAMILY!

Jackie: When we got married, we made a promise to each other that we would not forsake the other person for anyone or anything. I know a lot of other people don't abide by those values or live up to those vows. People say, "Well, we'll enter into this marriage, and if it works it works, and if not, not." For us, there is no divorce option. We agreed that we would each be who we said we would be. Marriage doesn't work when one person's one way and one person's the other.

Doug: Both sides must give a hundred percent for a marriage to work. Until I was ready to do that, it wasn't the right time.

Jackie: But if you are ready, it won't be hard. There'll be ups and downs. But it's not hard to be married to your soul mate. Doug had just gotten traded to Toronto, and I was elated and shocked and not sure what to expect. I'd been around the NBA for a while now, and I saw that players sometimes left their wives and families in their home cities, wherever they were. So I asked Doug, "Are we staying in Seattle?"

Doug: "No, you're coming with me to Toronto. We are a family now!"

Jackie: Not long after we moved to Toronto with Doug, there was a golf tournament with Isiah Thomas. He couldn't have been more friendly; he took pictures with everybody—it was great. I immediately felt welcome. It was scary at the same time, though, for me, being the new wife of a player. We decided that we wouldn't have any secrets from each other—past, present, or future. We confessed everything to each other that we had been through. We discussed all of our previous relationships. We decided there was no need for skeletons and surprises. I felt closer to him than ever, and the process strengthened our marriage.

I think the process of telling each other everything about our pasts made us become best friends. Now we could open up and share ourselves differently. It put us in a different realm. I was not just his wife but his soul mate. We could tell each other anything. Also, we were young, and Doug was an athlete—you know, basketball players can get a lot of women. They're tall and attractive, and the women just gravitate toward them. We went through that period where I was ready but he wasn't, but once we reached the confession level, now I knew this was for keeps.

He would never lie to me, in that time before we committed, but if I asked him questions, he'd say things to me with a smile like, "Don't concern yourself with that," "Don't mess in my business, Miss Jackie," or "I'm just gonna be like my dad. He never married and neither will I," or "That's only for a wife to ask. Key word: wife!"

But he tried to be respectful all the time, and I never saw him out with another girl. I'd send him treats, and poems and cards.

Doug: Before I asked my wife to marry me, I knew she was the only one for me. I found out after we were married that being faithful wasn't hard at all. It's about your focus and what really matters to you. We can relax together and have a good time and have fun. Unfortunately, people wouldn't take kindly to our being married, but that was in the future.

I'm a romantic at heart. I loved Luther Vandross and Teddy Pendergrass. When I met my wife, I knew in my gut ... this is the one. But I was always still telling myself, "Dad's not married. I'm not getting married. I'm single, and this is how I'm going to live my life." But deep down inside, I knew I wanted this. But there was the fear of the unknown. I was coming into life without a notebook on how to live life. I was just trying to figure it out. Outside I was trying to keep up the façade of "I'm never getting married." But inside, I really wanted it.

Jackie: Until that moment when he finally said, "Let's get married," I was sometimes saying to myself, "This is never going to happen." I would say the Serenity Prayer—"God, grant me the serenity to accept the things I cannot change"—just to stay optimistic. Sometimes when we were together, I'd even sign my name as Jackie Christie on things.

Doug: I'd cross it out and say, "Stop playing, girl!"

Jackie: Whenever I'd be weary, he'd write, "I love you, but I'm not sure what I want to do." He just hadn't figured it out yet. My decision was to love him regardless. It wasn't difficult to wait. And he always treated me like a lady. Christmases, Thanksgivings, or holidays were always special times we spent together.

Doug: My best friend Tyrone—his parents have been married a long time. So he grew up with more of a sense of security, because his father was there. When Jackie and I had a child, obviously, I loved her even before we were married, and I loved her even before we had a child. But once we had that child, I knew—this was my family. When we spent holidays together, I knew I loved the feeling. My quandary was how to make it work. If you're gonna do it, stand strong. That halfway thing doesn't work with me. But once I decided to commit, it wasn't a problem for me. Once we got married, I told Jackie to forget all about stuff I had said about not wanting to get married. That was just mumbo-jumbo talk, male ego talk. Really, I wanted to be married.

Jackie: Everything Doug just said sums up what I was going to say. He reminds me of a toddler—they get up, they fall back down two or three times, but when they're finally ready, they get up and keep walking. When he finally made the commitment to walk, he walked.

Doug: It wasn't a coincidence that we got married when I was traded to Toronto. By this time I knew how much I loved Jackie, how much I needed and wanted her with me. Things were going so well with the Raptors, with Isiah at the helm.

I know that I have someone special, and she knows she has someone special, and risking that is not even an option.

The feeling I have inside—it hasn't changed. And that's the part that keeps it fun. When you look at our backgrounds—I'm not talking about the socioeconomic level; I'm just talking about the fact that we both come from single-parent homes—it was really against the odds that we would find each other, commit, and live a life of Infinite Love.

Jackie: But we have.

Doug: Yes, we have. The best-known symbol of our relationship is the hand signal I give my wife when I'm playing. People don't know the story of how that came about, so we thought we'd share that with you.

Jackie: How it all started was, the first year we were married and the season began, I was sitting in the stands with our daughter Chantel. He looked at me and smiled, and I smiled back. I remember I thought, "Okay, I really hope they win tonight, but I think someone from our team needs to do something—and fast. Doug should drive to the hole, because he is good at it." So I started making these hand signs like with my fist balled up, and I would pat it on my head—silly, I know, but I didn't care, I wanted us to win. When he looked at me again and saw this, he looked a little confused. So I decided, okay, after the game we will talk, and then the next game he will know.

As soon as the disappointing loss was over, we talked about what I was doing and I said, "Next time if I do this, it's drive to the hole, and this is dunk it!" and so on. And he laughed and said, "Okay, honey, let's try next game." So we did.

And then after they won, he said, "Now, honey, I will give you a sign and you will have to figure this one out. Deal?"

"Sure," I said, confident I could do it. But, oh boy, was I surprised when he made me the "sign." And I said, "What the heck does that mean—two points, the two of us?" "What," I thought. I know I must have looked bewildered. He would not look at me through the whole game, only give me this sign, and I said to myself, "He is going to get it." Smiling at the secret sexiness of it all, I thought, "It's our secret. No one else knows but us," and it was very special. Whatever it meant, it was ours.

Doug: She didn't have a clue to what it meant, and I knew it so I had the satisfaction of her having to guess and wonder. It was sweet revenge for the signs she gave me only a game before and I had to wait.

Jackie: As soon as the game ended, I said, "Okay, big guy, what gives?" And he said, "It means I love you!" And I smiled and reached for his hand and said, "Thank you, honey. I love you, too!"

Doug: Soon, a reporter asked me what it meant, and I said it was something to my wife, that I'm saying I love her. And that all is good, no matter what. He said, "That's nice. Now why do you feel the need to have to do that?" I simply said, "Why do you breathe?" Well, you can probably imagine he didn't like my answer, but his question to me was dumb. It lacked realness, and I didn't take lightly to anyone questioning me sarcastically about my wife.

Jackie: Besides, why should he worry anyway, when the team began winning quite often and Doug's play was getting much attention from everyone around, including the media and commentators?

Doug: But lo and behold, the reporters did take notice of my sign to Jackie and began to talk more about it than basketball, as far as I was concerned.

Jackie: The comments and lies soon followed, but we just kept on living our life and decided that they would soon tire of the nonsense and all would be fine …

Doug: But not these guys … they had just begun! And once it came out that we were happily married, a lot of things changed. It seemed suddenly like I had a target on my back. Certain women that came around the team would try to flirt with me, which I ignored. And then one day I had to do an interview. The team and

I were doing great, playing well and moving forward, and this reporter seemed way too friendly, which I took offense to, because I always wanted to keep things professional, and it seemed to me she had something else in mind. So I kindly would change the subject if it was not on the beaten path of basketball. And she was offended.

I realized after this awkward interview that I needed to discuss this with team management, and I did just to avoid future situations. They were very supportive and told me that if I did not want to interview with her or anyone acting unprofessional, they had no problem with it. Now mind you, I did have a job to do, and part of it was to grant interviews with all sports media, and I had every plan to do just that. But she didn't seem to want it that way! It appeared that she wanted "more"—something that I definitely was not at all interested in giving her.

Jackie: My husband came home from practice and said he had done this interview that he mentioned earlier, and that she was a bit flirtatious and he had backed her off. Also, he had spoken to management and that they were supportive, and that if it did not stop, she would have to interview someone else. And of course, I agreed and felt that it would all work out.

Doug: The next time I was scheduled to do the interview with that station, my wife happened to be with me, since it was following a game we had won, and the same person was there to do the interview—with the same behavior. This time was her last, however, as I made it clear that I wanted no part of it, and my family and I went out to dinner that night to celebrate our victory and our newfound city of Toronto!

The days that followed were smooth, except for the occasional bump here or there with some of the media that had heard about the unfortunate encounters I had with that reporter, and they also took offense! You would have thought there was a campaign to spread hate and lies that began shortly after my run-in with the reporter. It was even suggested that I would not interview with women unless Jackie was present. We again ignored it and hoped for the best, and that it too would soon pass.

Jackie: But that would prove to be a very big mistake going forward!

Doug: Also, reporters were curious because there were so few married players at the time. We would leave hand in hand after the game, and they thought that to be odd since most of the guys kind of hung out a little afterwards and socialized. I just wanted to go home and be with my family.

Jackie: So when we would leave, we would see the glares from the media and thought, "Why are they so concerned with what a player does after his job is done?" All we were doing was what any other normal couple would do—we were going home ...

It was just a lot of pressure back then to deal with all the media's scrutiny of our marriage, but we just blocked it all out. We were and still are committed to each other, our marriage, and our family.

Doug: We had a toddler by this point, and we were living in a foreign country and trying to learn our way around at the same time. We also had a lot of responsibilities outside of basketball.

Jackie: Those first fabricated stories about how Doug and I had this really weird relationship, that I was crazy, among other things, that I controlled him—this was incredibly painful. Those stories were very hurtful. Suddenly I had gone from being just the girlfriend of an NBA player to a woman being attacked by the media every time I turned around. Before that, if I had been in the paper, it would have had to do with my modeling career. And now I was getting all this nonsense. My first instinct was to lash out. People were saying that Doug was henpecked. The whole thing was silly. My attitude was, "You're not saying anything positive." That's what I told the reporters. So early on they labeled me as the one wearing the pants. This is our marriage and ours alone, and we just want to live our lives. We don't need these untrue stories and hurtful little jokes, but if that's what they obviously had to do to feel good about themselves, so be it. We know the truth.

Doug: It was wild.

Jackie: Back then, the Raptors didn't have their own training facility. They would practice at a small college called Brendon College, on the outskirts of Toronto. Chantel and I would play in the little kids' room, or I would work out while Doug practiced with the team. There would be snow everywhere on the ground, it was cold, and I would have to bundle Chantel up every time we needed to go out. We were not used to the extremely cold weather, and we decided to make the best of it and do more things indoors to entertain our growing family!

Around that time, Isiah Thomas had begun negotiations to buy the team, but that deal fell through. Team ownership changed a time or two in a short period, and things began to become unstable as far as the team was concerned.

Also, we were dealing with extreme cruelty from some of the sports media. There were the sprinkles here and there of the nice stories about us that others chose to do, but the bad outweighed the good most of the time.

Doug: It was about this time that the new owners had decided to hire a new coach—not that there was anything wrong with the old one. In fact, we all really liked Darrell Walker a whole lot, so of course it was not good to see him leave. Anyway, they called a meeting with me because, at the time, I had been with the team the longest. Damon Stoudamire, one of my other good friends, had gone by now, too, so they asked my opinion about the assistant coach becoming our new head coach.

Jackie: Doug had talked to him on occasion, and he had shared with him his philosophy on how he would run the team, and it all sounded good. So when they asked Doug, he said, "Why not? He is here already, the team knows him, and he seems to have a pretty good plan."

Doug: So he had my vote, they hired him, and off we went. It was shortly after that, one day in practice, I sprained my ankle. In order for me to still be able to play and contribute to the team, I needed to stay warm by being out on the floor in the game for longer periods, which I was used to. And if I was taken in and out of the game, it allowed for my ankle to get cold and stiffen back up, therefore making it harder to play through the intense pain.

Jackie: It began to wreak havoc on his ankle, and I was NOT happy about it. He had given of himself to the team time and time again. Surely this new coach would understand.

Doug: I felt that the time was quickly approaching that I would need to have a conversation with him and work something out.

Jackie: Doug was under so much pressure—he didn't want to disappoint the team, the coach, the fans … heck, anyone. He wanted to be the best player he could and help the team win, hurt or not. So he changed his mind about having that conversation with the coach, after all. He would just wait and see what happened.

Doug: Up until this point I had been a constant in the starting lineup, and one day the coach called me into his office and said, "How would you feel if we don't start you?" I said, "I wouldn't like it, but you're the coach." What exactly was I supposed to say?

Was I happy? Hell, no! But was the team more important and could I take this opportunity and turn it into a positive as I have so many times in my career and life? "Yes," I thought.

Jackie: But mind you, there had been some bumpy times since this new coach came on board as headmaster! He had started to change. It was as though he had an issue of sorts with my husband!

And of course, I was so proud of Doug being the man that he is. He didn't take it personally. He just worked harder to heal his sprained ankle and cheered for the team. As I sat in the stands and watched how he was still supportive of the guys and happy for them, my heart swelled, for it just convinced me even more that I had made the right choice in the man that I married.

Doug: The irony is, I felt like I may have helped him get the job a little easier. I wasn't looking for anything in return—no special treatment or anything. I work for mine, always have and always will, but I was looking for strong leadership and good results for our team!

But, boy oh boy, was I wrong. The team began a slight decline and the coach was not happy in the least bit, and soon, it seemed, I would become his reason. I came to every practice and every game with one-hundred-percent tenacity, but he seemed to have another idea about me in his mind. And soon, Toronto, Canada, was not big enough for the two of us.

Jackie: Or the three of us, as I confronted him. I said, "I'm sorry, but you're not gonna hurt my husband. He was doing great until you came along. And what you're doing is not right."

Doug: Keep in mind that, in Canada, taxes are something like fifty percent. So we were spending a huge amount of money just to live there. We leased two apartments, right across the street from Air Canada Center, where the team played its NBA games—one for us and one for our mom, since she helps with baby-sitting duties, since we don't allow anyone but family to watch our kids.

Jackie: People assume that once you're in the NBA, you've got more money than you can possibly deal with. But back then, it sounds crazy, but when taxes are eating up half your income and the tax advice you are getting is not great, it's not the best situation. You see, every season we would move all of our clothes back home to the States with us. So you can imagine, also, the whole time maintaining three residences—two in Toronto and one in Seattle, our hometown.

It was off the hook, but all the while I knew our love was pure and strong, and we would endure through it all.

Doug: Back to the head coach. Around this time, the new owners of the team wanted to meet the two of us, so we went over to their home with our agent. The purpose of the dinner was to just smooth everything over, but now things went in the most bizarre direction. My agent said to the owners, "We just want to tell you that Doug has to be traded."

We tried not to look shocked—where was this coming from? We were under the impression that we were going to their home to talk about everything—and now this! I think my agent was trying to get me traded, and he had come up with the idea of just being very frank, that I was not happy and just wanted out. Anyway, that's what some of the newspapers were saying, so maybe he thought it would go over with the owners. But they didn't fall for it. They said, "It boils down to this. Doug has a contract and he has to uphold that contract." My agent gave me a look like, "It's okay, I know what I'm doing." He said, "My client demands a trade."

Jackie: Well, you can imagine the next two seasons playing there, right? Finally, they decided to trade Doug. Actually, I was okay with leaving Toronto. But I would miss it, as the city was great to us, and it was nothing personal toward Toronto.

Doug: There was more to the situation, though. I think everybody understands that the NBA has a lot of groupies, waiting outside the arena, at the hotel, wherever, just to meet the ballplayers. What I think a lot of people don't know is that some of those groupies actually end up getting jobs with some of the teams! It's not the teams' fault. It's not like they recruit these women. The women recruit the teams.

It is probably understood all around that these girls are going to end up having relationships with the players. I'll give you an example. Let's say you've got an autograph signing to do. Well, the team might send over an attractive girl to drive you in her car. She might be flirting or just really friendly. And then one thing leads to another and then you get caught up in that whole situation—something I didn't want anything to do with. If we were going to a signing, I would bring my wife with me and we would enjoy it together. After all, it shouldn't matter who the woman accompanying me is, right?

Jackie: Not so. Soon, that too was an odd Christie thing the media didn't like. The woman doing the so-called errands for the players didn't like it, either. Luckily, the Toronto Raptors had no problems with my joining Doug at events and even encouraged family participation.

Doug: Besides, why did I need some female driving me anywhere when I've had my driver's license since I was sixteen?

Jackie: And remember, he's the guy with the target on his back. Tight skirts and low-cut tops were the norm. And don't let the players have a team meeting, because the girls will come dressed to kill. The times when they would make their play was never easy. Tip—the guys were always prey!

Doug: Even though the reporters sometimes gave me a hard time about Jackie, the players never did. They respected my relationship with my wife, and even though the girly talk went on in the locker room, it didn't concern me and they knew that.

Jackie: I felt really special when Isiah Thomas, the team's general manager, told Doug to have me fly with the team on the road trips. So, as I had been flying on a separate plane to each city and meeting him there, this made it much more convenient. Besides, I made eighty percent of the trips anyway and got to spend quality time with my husband.

Doug: Isiah was very good to me and to my family.

Jackie: All the strife that the media tried to put us through in Toronto only galvanized us and made us stronger, made us realize it was us against the world. It was like a game to them to try and break us, but little did they know they were wrong.

Doug: Well, I was being traded to Sacramento from Toronto after nearly five years. It was time to go and it was a huge blessing, mainly because it was closer to home, but also I felt I could help this new team and start a new chapter in our life away from the sports media spotlight of hate and fabricated stories and one-sided comments, and bring my family to a happier situation.

Jackie: That it did, babe. That it did.

Doug: And it's a good thing, because we'd have to get a lot stronger in order to deal with what was coming next!

FIVE

~

THE DREAM TEAM

Jackie: Leaving Sacramento was like leaving home. The organization, the players, the coaches, the fans—they were all fantastic. It was the greatest experience of Doug's career, and it was certainly the highlight of my time with Doug in the NBA.

Doug: It was a very family-oriented team. From the coaches to the players to the front office, everyone kind of jived. It was wonderful, start to finish. The first day we found out we were going to be traded from Toronto to Sacramento, my wife and I were very excited to see our new city.

Jackie: To be honest, I didn't know what to expect. But it turned out better than either of us could have imagined.

Doug: It was a good team and a fantastic situation for me. I fit in right away with the guys on the team and with the coaching staff. I saw that the staff was really teaching basketball—something that doesn't always happen at the NBA level—how to move without the ball, how to cut. The whole experience in Sacramento was heaven on earth for a basketball player because it was so easy—it was like playing an All-Star game every night.

When you watch the All-Star game on TV, the players never seem to be thinking about who they're going to pass to, because they know that whoever gets the ball will be able to do something smart with it. That's how it was on the Kings back then. We really had a chance to win every single game. And the fans were amazing. It felt like they had a vested interest in the team like alumni do when it comes to their universities. Rick Adelman was the coach, and the other team he had coached, the Portland Trailblazers, was also a team in a city that had no other professional sports teams. In both Sacramento and Portland, the Kings and the Trailblazers are the only pro game around. The cities are basketball oriented and they love everything about their teams. So that was really fantastic, also. The thing about us was that we didn't look like the world's greatest team or the world's most disciplined team. We were so loose during our warm-ups that I think other teams half the time would underestimate us. They'd think, "Who in the hell are these guys? We are going to beat the crap out of them!" And then we'd come out on the floor and just beat them. It was incredible. When it was time to focus and play the game, we would lock in and compete. That's the fine line—some teams get all tied up in how well they're doing, whether they're winning or losing. But we were never like that. We just went out there, had fun, and won games.

Jackie: I couldn't explain it any better. That was Sacramento.

Doug: When you break down the team, you see just how amazing it was. First, you had **RICK ADELMAN** *(right)*, who is definitely the best coach I've ever played for in the NBA.

Then you had **PETE CARRILL** *(left)*, "Coachie" (one of my all-time favorite people), the assistant coach, who

had excelled in the college game at Princeton. Coachie had the innate ability to simplify the game. He would give me advice that absolutely changed the way I played, like "Watch the guy in front of you, because he'll show you where to go. He goes right, you go left. He stops, you go." Could it be that simple? Yes.

Then you had CHRIS WEBBER— "C-Webb" *(right)*—I would go into battle with Chris any day or night. Webb was one of those cats you meet once in a lifetime. Some people didn't realize just how valuable he was to the team and how good

he was. At the end of the night you could glance at the box score, and there would be Chris leading every category—thirty points, nine assists, twelve rebounds, a couple of blocks, a couple of steals. Simply, Webb made everyone better, which is the sign of a truly great player.

Jackie: He was also one of our strongest supporters. We have so much love and respect for Chris.

Doug: **JASON WILLIAMS** *(right)* —he was just plain fun. He'd flip the ball to me and yell, "Shoot it, Shorty!" He's just a great guy to be around. Jason was definitely misunderstood. In my opinion, Jason was one of those people who got a bad rap. And he was a joy to  play with as a teammate. He always made the mood lighthearted on the bus or on the team plane. He  could just say the funniest, most outlandish things to make everybody laugh.

Then, from the country of Serbia-Montenegro, **VLADE DIVAC** *(left)* was one of the first ambassadors for the game around the world. He knows the game so well—all the little angles, how to take advantage. (Not to mention, he's the luckiest man in the world.) Whenever he was open, I'd throw the ball to him. I knew he'd get an assist, get a basket, or finish the play.

The most eccentric guy of the bunch—big **SCOT POLLARD** *(next page, left),* a warrior. He never complained if he

wasn't playing a lot. He would just go out there and fight and fight and fight. We could always count on Scot's hair to distract the other team, so they wouldn't see us coming!

Then there was our other Serbian, **PEJA STOJAKOVIC** *(below)* — a true

assassin. He was one of the best pure shooters I've ever seen in the game. It took me a while to figure out that he just saw something different when he looked at the basket. It's kind of like the way Picasso saw something different when he painted. Peja had Picasso's eye for shooting.

Next came **BOBBY JACKSON** *(left and below)*, my one-on-one buddy. We had a love/hate relation-

ship—we'd go at each other all the time, but we loved each other to death. We'd play one-on-one to tighten our game and we'd end up getting hurt banging heads in practice. The coach would be like, "What's wrong with you guys?" But that was Bobby, never backing down. As soon as he hit the court, he'd be going nine million miles an hour.

And then you've got "Mr. Team Dime," **MIKE BIBBY** *(next page, top left)*. We called him Team Dime because he wore number ten and always traveled with his entourage. They were some serious gentlemen in that entourage. They didn't have to be big to be serious. You can tell when somebody's

serious. No question, they were just good guys. When we went on the road it could be hostile, because we were beating everyone. But we never had to worry, because Team Dime would be looking after the players' wives and families and making sure all was good. Mike fit right in when he joined us. He's a solid shooter and a solid basketball player. He came in and helped us at a time when they traded Jason, and he kept everything clicking.

And finally we have brother **HEDO TURKOGLU** *(right)*. He was the biggest jokester of all the European players. He came from Turkey, and every arena in which we played had its own Turkish section rooting for him. "HEDO! HEDO!" they'd chant.

The year that Hedo left, a part of me went with him.

Jackie: And what about **DOUG CHRISTIE** *(next page)*?

Doug: I was the defensive player that allowed our scorers to do their thing—out of the perimeter players, I would guard the greatest offensive threat. Since I didn't have to worry about scoring all that much, I would do whatever was necessary on any given night, from setting people up to getting a few baskets—whatever we needed. I felt blessed to be able to do that.

That team was a real melting pot of basketball—color lines were never an issue. We had Europeans, white guys, black guys. We were all one team.

We had a lot of injuries, and that's when the word "team" would really come into play. Turkoglu would step in when Stojakovic would go down, for example, but the train never stopped. We just kept on winning. Whoever came in would fit in. When C-Webb went down, it hurt us so much because of what he brought to the game. We were still kicking without him, but maybe not smashing.

In short, my years with Sacramento represented my happiest time in the NBA. It was definitely the place where I learned the most. I don't think we ever lost three games in a row more than a couple of times. That's because Rick Adelman was a player's coach. He understood what the player's body was going through over the course of the long NBA season. If we had back-to-back games, we would never practice on the third day, even if the Lakers were our next opponent. That's something that the good teams know how to do—create schedules that allow people to rest and recover, and make all important plans with their families. When we did practice, Rick would start us with drills. We worked on footwork, passing, cutting, and shooting. Then all of a sudden, our competitive juices would kick in, and we'd be scrimmaging like crazy. That's one thing that we did—scrimmage a lot. So when we got into the games, it looked like what we were doing was second nature, because it truly was second nature by then. Poetry in motion! Sacramento was a smorgasbord—we had all different types of players, all different types of styles. It worked, and that's what was so special about it.

Jackie: That's why it was so disappointing for Doug to be traded from that team.

Doug: As an athlete, it was heartbreaking. When you're injured, you can't defend yourself. We were oh-so-close to winning a championship—that was our goal. I remember telling myself we ran into a dynasty. The whole League ran into Jordan and the Bulls all those glorious years. We ran into the Lakers—nothing to hang our heads about. There were great battles, drama, not to mention some of the best basketball seen in recent memory ... and yeah, even a fight or two. You had to love it!

Of all the teams playing today, the current Phoenix Suns team ('06-'07) is closest to our team in Sacramento in terms of its diversity. They're from all over the world and they blend in beautifully. (You look at them warming up, and they don't look like much. But once they're out there on the floor, they're coming at you in waves.) You've got Steve Nash, whose attitude is, "We're out here to win, so whoever is open gets the ball." You see them applauding each other, giving each other high-fives. Guys were encouraging each other even when they messed up. On some teams, you don't see that—you see tension when guys make mistakes. I don't see that on the

Phoenix team. Also, on the best teams, everyone knows their roles. Everybody knows exactly what is expected of them, and they're okay with playing those roles. No one heads out to the floor saying, "It's all about me tonight." It's a team effort, and they all make it work.

On San Antonio, you've got a similar situation. Tony Parker, Manu Ginobili, Tim Duncan—all kinds of great players. This is another team where the superstar can sacrifice his own numbers for the betterment of the whole. It's just beautiful to behold.

That's why I loved Sacramento—guys played together as a team, contributed, and made amazing things happen. There's only one bad memory of our time in Sacramento. A former employee of the Kings decided to bring a lawsuit against the team, and against the two of us. The events involving this individual overshadowed our time in Sacramento for a short period. As the lawsuit she filed was bogus, it was eventually dropped … but not before we went through torment and harassment. And as usual, the events were twisted in the media. We signed a confidentiality agreement, so we have to be circumspect about the details. It was very unfortunate that we had to go through that, but it just helped to strengthen our already unbreakable bond.

Jackie: The funny thing about the situation was that we had never done anything wrong. And even though we constantly proclaimed our innocence, a few reporters still wanted to believe—and report—otherwise. We knew that at the end of the day—

Doug: Which took one and a half years to complete!

Jackie: —we knew that we would be vindicated. And

anyway, we had a lot of support from the many beautiful people of Sacramento, California, and from the team who knew it was just not true.

Doug: Overall, Sacramento was the highlight of my career. To be blessed to have Jackie and our family there with me to share in it was the greatest. So when we were traded from Sacramento to Orlando, and that part of our life got pulled out from underneath us, it was very difficult on our entire family.

Jackie: Some of the sports media were there to make their usual comments.

Doug: Stories were written that I couldn't take getting traded. That's not true. Yes, we would truly miss Sacramento, the whole city. It had become our second home. We will always have love for Sacramento. But we all know it's a business, and you do have close relationships that you build up at the same time. In Sacramento, we truly had a family situation. Unfortunately, we weren't able to get over the hump and win the ring. Nonetheless, all the experiences we had along the way made it worthwhile. And the fans were incredible. When you went up to shoot, you could feel all the air sucked out of the arena. Or you'd be looking up at the ceiling while the floor was trembling, thinking, "Is the roof going to pop off?"

It wasn't just the playoffs. Even during the regular season, when we were really rolling, the fans would just lose their minds. When Phil Jackson came to Sacramento, he would put earplugs in his ears, but they couldn't have made much of a difference. The noise in that arena was so deafening that you could feel it in your chest.

Jackie: All good things must come to pass, I guess.

Doug: Yes. Leaving Sacramento was hard. I'm glad I didn't know what was in store for me in my next few NBA stops. God doesn't give you more than you can handle. That's a good thing, considering what was coming.

SIX

~

ON THE MOVE

Doug: It all started in Sacramento. I was playing well and it
            was a great situation for me, no question about that.
            Then one morning I woke up and found that my left
            heel was hurting.

Jackie: I thought that if he just stretched enough the pain
            would go away, but it was much more than that.

Doug: We were in the playoffs. We had just beaten Utah and
            the pain was increasing daily. Then we started the
            second round against the Dallas Mavericks. The pain
            grew so much that I almost couldn't even walk. I had
            plantar fasciitis, an inflammation of the tendon that
            connects the heel to the bone. It's hard to walk or run
            with that condition, let alone play NBA basketball.

            The first two games I got a lot of treatment and
            was able to play, but it was becoming unbearable,
            and I realized that if I was going to continue playing,
            I would need a shot of cortisone to kill the pain. So
            now it's game 4 at home in Sacramento. We're about
            to head out onto the floor for pre-game warm-ups. In

my head I knew that the pain was too much. As soon as I approached the basket, I knew it wasn't going to work. So I ran off the floor to the training room to see the doctor, and he gave me about eight or nine shots on the bottom of my foot. Immediately my foot went numb. As soon as I stepped down, it felt as though I was walking on a tightrope. I spent the rest of the warm-up trying to figure out how to get my balance.

Somehow I played well in that series and we won, and then we lost a heartbreaking game 7 to Minnesota. So our season was over and we headed back to Seattle. The team trainer told me I'd be fine, just get some rest.

I did, but there was no improvement. So I decided to give my physical therapist, Bill O'Grady, a call. He keeps my body tuned up in the off season. After my telling him what was happening, he said, "I know a doctor by the name of Andy Cole, who would be a good person to advise you on what would be best for you."

So I called Dr. Cole and he ordered an MRI (a high-tech x-ray) before my coming in to see him. We got the results and took them back in to see Dr. Cole. He put the photos up on the light board, and the first thing he said was, "You need surgery." I nudged my wife like, "I can't believe he's saying this!" (But oh, how right he was!) He then went on to explain, "You've got two bone spurs, which aren't that big of a problem. But they are impeding the ability of your ankle to fully flex. So the plantar fasciitis is a by-product of your bone spurs. If you don't get them removed, your problems will only increase."

So we went home and called the Sacramento trainer, Pete Youngman. I told him about the MRI and what Dr. Cole had said, and he tried to reassure me, saying, "You'll be fine, just rest, and if not, we'll try some other options." So I did, but to no avail. Now summer is over and it's time to go back to Sacramento for training camp. I hadn't worked out at all and wasn't ready to begin the season. The team was going to China, but I wasn't. Instead, I had to stay behind and get a new treatment, electroshock therapy, on the trouble spot. The procedure is performed with a device that hits you with 2,000 volts of electricity in about fifteen spots. The theory behind the treatment is that it treats inflammation with inflammation. I know it sounds crazy. But I went along with the treatment.

Now the team's in China and I'm home, trying to get myself ready for the season. My wife is doing all she can to help me. Once I felt better, I began walking on the treadmill and then jogging, but I couldn't feel anything on the bottom of my foot. I didn't realize at the time that, thanks to the electroshock therapy, the symptoms were gone, but the problem was still there. When the season began, I was put in my starting role with the team, but I wasn't as explosive as usual.

Now we're on a road trip and the last city was New Orleans. My wife and I are talking business and basketball, as we usually do after games, and I say, "Babe, something's not right; they are not playing me the same. Something is going on. I think they might make a trade."

Jackie: I agreed—things didn't look right.

Doug: I'm usually in there at the deciding time of the game.

They know I'm going to get a steal, or do something to try to help the team win. But my minutes were getting funky. I wasn't being inserted at crunch time. The reality was that I was only capable of playing at about seventy percent of my normal abilities. It didn't matter. I felt we were going to get traded.

Then the next day, after getting back from New Orleans, I was on the cell phone with my agent, who's explaining the situation with the team. He's telling me, "Don't worry, there's no trade going to happen." As those words roll off his tongue, our home phone rings. My wife answers it and hands it to me. It's Geoff Petrie, Sacramento's general manager. He sounded a little choked up, not like his normal self. His words echoed: "Doug, this is the hardest phone call I've had to make …," he paused, "… we've just traded you to Orlando."

I tried to be strong and I thanked him for his call. My wife looked at me and knew something was wrong. My eyes welled up with tears as I held them back the best I could. In one 45-second conversation, it was all over. The phone began to ring with well-wishers; the players started coming by one by one, which was the hardest, starting with Webb (Chris Webber) and me looking at each other, not knowing exactly what to say, all your feelings on your face. Then try to explain to your children that this isn't your "home" any longer. It's just hard. We are a family and through it all we are together. The adversities will always come, but we hold each other tight and know that we can depend on one another.

So now we've got to hustle, because we had to get everything packed and get to Orlando in forty-eight hours. I was a bit worried. Even though I was healthy, I just wasn't able to do what I had done in the past. My ankle was hurting; the bottom of my foot was still numb. I'm saying to myself, this isn't good. We arrived in Orlando. I was taking so many pain relievers, just to give them whatever I could, that I was developing stomach problems. Then, in a game against Indiana just before the All-Star break, I sprained my ankle within the first ten seconds of the game.

After the break, I returned and still tried to play. My ankle wasn't getting any better. I knew all the pain medication couldn't be doing my body any good. So I decided that now was the time to get surgery.

Jackie: Doug's a warrior, but he knew the situation was serious. He couldn't keep on playing like that.

Doug: After I made my mind up to get surgery, I was really feeling terrible. I ended up missing a practice and the next game. The team was displeased, and the media had a field day with that and reported that I was absent from the team. I then rejoined the team on a road trip to New York, where I sat down for a meeting with John Weisbrod, the general manager, and Otis Smith, the head of basketball operations. I explained that I needed to get surgery. They were both very understanding. They weren't happy, because they had just traded for me. But this was the result of an accumulation of years of injuries. Normally, I would do anything for the team—if you're going to make it in the NBA, you're going to sacrifice a lot for "the team." But now I had to do something for myself if I was going to continue to be a professional basketball player. We returned to Seattle for the surgery.

Well, you know some of the sports media. They used this as a perfect opportunity to attack me. Mike Bianchi of the *Orlando Sentinel* wrote some highly critical and hurtful stories about me. A year later, he was still describing what had happened to me as a "phantom injury." When I finally went in for the surgery, the team sent a trainer as an observer to make sure it all went well.

Before I went in I showed the doctor one particular spot that was giving me the most pain. He said, "Nothing showed up on the MRI in that area, but I promise while you are out I will take an exploratory look." Thank God he did. He pulled out two pieces of bone embedded in my tendon that had calcified. Each was at least one millimeter in diameter.

The surgery was successful, my ankle was healing, and I was feeling fantastic. I was home, laid up, recovering, but I knew I was on the comeback trail. Shortly after my surgery, we decided to do our own press conference via satellite from Seattle to demonstrate the reality of the injury, and to show the naysayers that I had been honest about the whole thing.

John Weisbrod, the G.M., came to Seattle to talk with me face-to-face, to reassure me that I was still welcome in Orlando and that my return would be smooth. The day he arrived, I was still on crutches and the surgery was still quite recent. He was able to see for himself everything that my family and I had gone through. He understood that his player truly was injured, and he was very humble and apologetic about how we had been treated in Orlando. He offered no guarantees about how the media would respond to my return, but that wasn't an issue for me, as we were used to the media and their obsession with tearing us down. My main concern was getting myself healed up, so I could contribute. I explained to John that it would be a long rehabilitation process, and he said he understood. I was not going to be able to play through this pain as I had done before. I would need time to recover.

He left with the understanding that I would think it over, and we would talk the next week, but I admit that I felt better that he made the cross-country trip from Orlando to Seattle to reassure me about my future with the team. I talked with my wife after he left, and we were both very excited about my returning to Orlando, this time with me being healthy.

Not a week later, we were shocked to turn on the TV and discover that John had resigned.

Jackie: Doug was very concerned, because he was unsure of what was to come. The very person who had come to reassure him had just resigned.

Doug: The coaching position and the general manager position were both suddenly vacant. My thoughts centered on, "Where is this team headed?"

Jackie: As the days passed, Doug continued to rehab. We went to his appointments three times a week and he followed all of the doctor's instructions. Every day, he was getting stronger. The summer was nearing its end and it would be time to return to Orlando soon. Since Doug hadn't heard anything from the Magic, he called Otis Smith, the head of basketball operations.

In their friendly conversation, they spoke candidly about Doug's return.

Doug: I had thought a lot about the situation since Weisbrod had resigned, and it became increasingly apparent that I needed more time to get back to be one hundred percent of the player they had traded for. Otis understood my position and we discussed whether I would be returning. By the conversation's end, Otis told me that he would explore my other options and get back to me. The team was planning to make some moves that summer and he would see what he could do.

I was optimistic after the phone call that we would be able to work something out. I shared this information with my agent shortly thereafter and he began negotiating a buyout with Otis—I would forfeit a part of my salary and would not return to the Orlando Magic. And just like that, my turbulent time in Orlando was over. And now I could focus on getting healthy.

Fortunately, my career wasn't over. There are some outstanding teams in the NBA, and to play for any of them is a dream come true. There are plenty of players in the League who have spent their entire careers, despite their talent, playing for teams that were not yet championship caliber. So when you look at a team with the makeup of the Dallas Mavericks, you say to yourself, "Wow, imagine playing for them."

Jackie: That's what Doug would say when we would watch games on television.

Doug: Dallas had a new coach, Avery Johnson, and they became interested in me. My agent explained that I

Jackie: recently had surgery and my ankle was still a bit sore. Doug's agent said that Dallas wanted to send a private plane to pick us up and have us meet Mark Cuban—the owner of the Mavericks—and some of the Dallas brass. Then some of the plans changed and Mark wasn't able to make it. So Avery Johnson, the head coach, and Don Nelson Jr., the general manager, came to our home in Seattle.

Once we got the preliminaries out of the way, they came to their main concern. "We have to ask you," they began. "Do you still have the fire to play basketball?"

"By all means, yes," I said. "I absolutely do. I've been on a long rehab trail and I'm feeling much better."

That answer satisfied them—they knew I was being honest and that I wasn't trying to pretend my rehab was complete. "We know you are a defensive specialist," they told me. "You'll mentor other guys; we'll start you. It'll be great."

Jackie: When I heard those words, I was thinking, "God has come down on the porch and blessed this whole house!"

Doug: As the conversation continued, they told us that a gentleman would be hired as a "personal concierge" to handle all of our needs, from game tickets to air travel. We were like, "Wow, great!" They told me, "You just come and focus on basketball."

Jackie: Donnie Nelson said, "Dallas is a very family-oriented city. I'm sure you guys will be pleased."

I thought, "We're finally home!"

We talked about what happened before. They assured us there wouldn't be any such distractions in Dallas. We were comfortable and ready to embrace the city. They left without a definite answer—they wanted us to take our time and make our decision. But as soon as we shut the door, we knew what our decision would be. There were other teams also expressing interest, but Dallas was our choice.

Doug: It was perfect—we're going to Texas! So we started making plans to go. The day my wife and I arrived in Dallas for the Mavs' press conference my heart was overjoyed, as I was going to be a Dallas Maverick.

This was a team we had played so many times before when I was with the Kings, and I knew they were an up-and-coming powerhouse. I had watched their playoff run the season before. I said to my wife, "I could really help them—they are really good! I'd fit in!" So you can imagine me sitting next to Mark Cuban, one of the most celebrated owners in the game. Knowing his passion for his team, I thought, "Wow, this will be special."

We flew back to Seattle on a natural high. I was ecstatic because I could get back to competing. I would be playing alongside the likes of Dirk Nowitzki, Jason Terry, and Jerry Stackhouse, amongst others, and I anticipated us winning a lot of ball games. Our kids were also looking forward to moving to Dallas and wanted to know if they could have their own room.

Of course we said yes, but first we had to find a home. Our time frame was short as the season was quickly approaching. We needed to be situated so that I could go to work with a clear mind, knowing my family was settled. As luck would have it, we found a home that fit us to a tee!

Jackie: The home was beautiful. It had a nice backyard and we immediately began to put our own stamp on it.

Doug: My main concern was security and location for my family, and our new home had both.

Jackie: Life was good!

Doug: With the exception of my wife's squealing when she saw the occasional giant "water bug"! Back home we call them roaches, but we soon found out they're common in Dallas. No matter who you are or where you live, you are going to have a water bug or two.

Jackie: Those giant bugs … they took some real getting used to, I must say! Sometimes my mom and our kids would pile into one room upstairs, afraid of the water bugs. Doug would always be able to comfort us, even though he found it hilarious!

Doug: Gotta find the humor in it, babe.

Jackie: Yeah, right!

Doug: Actually, Dallas is one of the most desirable cities to visit or to live in from the perspective of NBA players. The restaurants are great, and that famous Texas hospitality always lives up to its high expectations.

Jackie: Whenever the schedule for the new season revealed when we were going to Dallas, you can bet that's a date I circled on my calendar.

Doug: So here we were in Dallas, Texas. The kids were in school and we were settling in.

Jackie: I immediately signed up at the local acting school and we were learning our way around the city. Doug had started going to the gym at night to get prepared for training camp, and I would go with him.

Doug: We also would take my buddy Tyrone with us, too, so he and I could play one-on-one.

Jackie: We would be in the gym from eight to eleven p.m.

most nights. Remember, he had not played since his ankle surgery and he wanted to get in shape.

Doug: It was all good until the first week of training camp, when my ankle really started to get sore. I tried to tell myself it would loosen up. My wife would massage it for me and get salts for me to soak in from the local health food store. But the pain lingered on. The Mavericks' trainer, who was very knowledgeable in sports medicine, would treat it for me, and soon the pain lessened. It didn't go away, but it was more bearable.

Jackie: Doug continued to work out and get treatment to prepare for the up-and-coming season.

Doug: Unfortunately, my ankle wasn't fully healed. Besides, there was the same old nonsense off the court. The team understood that I wasn't all the way back physically, and they knew I'd give everything I had to give. But my best that fall wasn't anything like what they had hoped for, or what I had hoped for. So after seven games, I went back to Seattle to get more treatment, but I still wasn't my old self. After speaking with the Dallas management, we agreed to a parting of the ways.

Jackie: I had made some friends in that short amount of time in Dallas, and the kids loved the city. So it was a disappointment for all of us.

Doug: I spent the rest of the year rooting for them and getting my ankle in shape. Man, it was hard watching them in the Finals, thinking about how much fun playing with them would have been. But I guess it wasn't meant to be.

Jackie: We sent Mark Cuban and Avery Johnson emails wishing them good luck in the Finals, and that we were rooting for them.

Doug: It's kind of ironic. My wife and I had seen Michael
         Jordan in Los Angeles at an event the summer after
         my surgery, and he told me, "Make sure you take
         your time coming back. It takes a lot longer to heal,
         the older you get."

         Oh, how I wish that I would have heeded his
         words instead of trying to be Superman! Although
         these two stops, Orlando and Dallas, didn't turn out
         the way we had hoped, it was a great experience all
         in all. Back to the drawing board of getting healthy
         and being in tip-top shape, as I would need to be
         for what was to come.

SEVEN

~

THE OPPORTUNITY

Doug: There are thirty teams in the NBA and fewer than half have winning records. By the fall 2006, I had fourteen years in the League and had been honored several times with All-League defensive awards. When I worked out with the Seattle SuperSonics at the beginning of the season, it looked as though we had found a home, although that turned out not to be the case. After things didn't work out with the SuperSonics, I had plenty of time to work out and to be with my family ... and to wonder why not many other teams had come calling.

   Had some of the management of the teams for which I had previously played put out a negative vibe about me? Or, had the unflattering comments in the media about my wife and me, and our marriage, proven sufficient to make teams think that I would be more of a liability than an asset?

   It was frustrating, but it was just something I had to live with. I continued to work out every day and I felt stronger and stronger. The one good thing that had come from my brief sojourn with the SuperSonics was my renewed confidence—I was back! My ankle was fully rehabilitated, and if anything, I could play better than ever. I knew I had the ability to be useful to an NBA team, if given the opportunity.

Jackie: And then the Clippers called.

Doug: The 2006-2007 Los Angeles Clippers were a highly talented group of ballplayers who, for various reasons, had not been achieving the success that most people had predicted for them. The year before, they had shocked the sporting world, especially in their home city of L.A., by going further in the playoffs than did the former world-champion Lakers.

So everybody thought that the Clippers would come out of the gate stronger than ever, building on their success from the previous season. While they started strongly, they faltered as the long NBA season wore on. So they began to look outside for help.

They tried a couple of players on 10-day contracts, but these players either failed to mesh with the team or failed to contribute in the way that management and ownership had hoped. So then they took an interest in me.

Jackie: We were in the process of moving to Los Angeles anyway, because much of our business interests are in L.A. and it was disruptive to our family for us to be flying back and forth between Seattle and L.A. so often. So once again, when the Clippers expressed an interest in Doug, it was hard not to get excited. If we moved to L.A. part-time, Doug could work on the court with the Clippers and off the court I would handle our business endeavors. It would have been perfect!

Doug: "Would have been" is the operative phrase, I'm sad to say. But anyway, there's a call from the Clippers. My agent says they want me to come in and work out for them. I say, "Great! Set it up and I'll be there!"

The night before my big workout, I couldn't sleep. I'm thinking, "Have I worked out hard enough? Will the work that I put in pay off?" I imagine I got around four hours of sleep!

Before I knew it, the phone rang and there was a voice on the other end saying, "Mr. Christie, your limo is downstairs, waiting." I met my agent in the lobby and entered the limo. My agent told me the workout would be held at the home of a close friend of head coach Mike Dunleavy. I know what you're thinking … a workout at someone's house? But the someone was a wealthy businessman with the perfect replica of the Lakers court at Staples Center … in his home! He had championship banners, retired names on the wall … the whole nine yards. It was unbelievable! I've never seen anything quite like it in a private residence.

Then I looked down at the end of the court, and there's the legend Elgin Baylor, the general manager of the Clippers. So I said to myself, "They must be serious if Elgin's here."

My agent and I walked down and exchanged pleasantries. Elgin informed us that Coach Dunleavy was running a little behind but would be joining us shortly. So I looked at Elgin and gestured to the court, as if to say, "May I … shoot?" He replied, "By all means!"

So I started shooting to loosen myself up. I was saying to myself, "Okay, I'm feeling pretty good." Ten minutes went and in walked the coach. He greeted me and said, "Whenever you're ready, we can get started." "I'm ready now!" I told him.

Coach Dunleavy then explained what the workout would entail. He wanted shots from all angles on the court, off screens, off the dribble, a full display of basketball and athletic skill. I nodded and said, "No problem!" He had me shoot ten shots from every spot on the floor. As soon as he passed me the ball, my first shot felt perfect. Swish!

They wanted to sign me.

Jackie: The first word we received from Doug's agent was that they wanted to sign him to a contract for the remainder of the season.

Doug: Then when I got home, I got a call from my agent. He informed me that they weren't trying to sign me for the rest of the season—they just wanted me to sign a 10-day contract. I should explain that NBA teams have the right to give a player an on-the-court audition in the form of a 10-day contract. This gives the player a chance to prove himself and also to see how well he fits in with the chemistry of the team. If he does well in the first 10-day contract, the team can sign him to a second one. If he does well after the second one, the team has to make a commitment and sign him for the rest of the season, or let him go. There's no such thing as a third 10-day contract.

The thing about these contracts is that they're really appropriate for players with whom the team is truly uncertain. It's a way of making a minimal investment or commitment to a player and yet having the opportunity to see how he performs under the pressure of NBA games. It was somewhat surprising to me that the Clippers wanted to sign me to a 10-day contract instead of signing me for the remainder of the season. It seemed odd because, after fourteen years in the League, and after the tryout they had seen, what more did they need to know?

Jackie: It's a question of respect.

Doug: You could say that. I had to question whether the Clippers really respected my game. That's really the way you handle individuals who have far less experience in the League. I was disappointed, and I told my agent to tell them, "Thanks, but no thanks."

Jackie: The next day, Doug's agent called me. It appeared he wanted me to convince Doug to accept the offer. That's not my role, I explained. It's his career—I'm happy to give him input and feedback, but it's not my role to convince him. He knows what he wants to do.

Doug: Then the coach, Mike Dunleavy himself, calls. He told me that he was thirty-six and coming back from an injury at one point in his own NBA career. He said that he knew it could be scary, but he hoped I would join the team.

"I just don't feel I'm a 10-day player," I told him.

Mike was very diplomatic. He said, "The only reason we're asking you to sign a 10-day contract is because you haven't played for a year and you're coming back from surgery."

Well, I felt honored, to say the least, that he would call himself and ask. And Jackie was okay with it so I said, "What the heck, we're together no matter what happens. This is just another life experience." So I decided to give it a shot.

Jackie: I just wanted Doug to be able to play. He had worked so hard to get healthy again. I was touched by Coach Dunleavy's call.

Doug: Within forty-eight hours, we were in Los Angeles. There was a shoot-around and Coach Dunleavy told me what time to be there. He said he would have his secretary send a car and e-mail the itinerary. Unfortunately, by the time I got to the gym, they were already watching film. I was late for my first day. It was just an unfortunate way to get things started. Everybody else is sitting there watching film and I'm like, "Hey, how you guys doing? Sorry I'm late!"

It was awkward, but everybody was cool. We had a walk-through and I stayed after to run through some plays.

Jackie: We were happy and excited. We wanted to just forget about the past and have a new beginning with the Clippers.

We arrived at the arena for the first game. I kissed Doug goodbye as he entered the locker room, and off to the wives' lounge I went to meet the other families and wait for the game to start.

Doug: I only got to play about two minutes, but that was okay. "They've got to work me into their system," I'm thinking. But then, when I get to the tunnel, I discover that they're not letting my wife and my agent into the area where she usually meets me. I'm like, "What's happening now?"

Jackie: Typically, there's a behind-the-scenes area where players' wives, girlfriends, friends, and family wait for players to emerge from the locker room. But they're not letting us in that area. We can see that there are people waiting outside the locker room entrance. I'm thinking to myself, "Please, don't let it all be starting all over again."

Fortunately, Doug's agent happened to be standing there and was able to straighten it out, so it was not a big deal.

Doug: Almost immediately, the team goes on a 12-day, 7-game road trip. I get the word that there's no problem, that Jackie can come along on the team plane, as the Clippers allow family members to travel with the team, which is a very good thing. Upon our arrival at the airport, Mike Dunleavy set us at ease. He gave us a genuinely warm feeling when he met my wife for the first time.

Jackie: We got onto the plane and sat down to relax for a bit before Doug headed to the front of the plane, where the players sit, to get comfortable with the team. The players always sit up front, the coaches and management in the middle, and the players' families and friends in the back. There really is a nice family feeling. I especially liked Daisy, Elton Brand's mother. She made me feel comfortable, and I admired her love and support for her son.

Doug: The highlight of the trip was the game in Philadelphia, where I had a steal that turned into a lay-up, which led to a seventeen-to-two Clippers run. The good thing was that I had begun to prove not just to the Clippers but to the entire NBA that I could still play. It was incredibly gratifying. Yet, at the same time, I'm getting no indication either way whether the Clippers are going to sign me for the rest of the season, or just let me go. I was enjoying playing with the guys on the team, and I really liked the coaching staff. Jackie had made friends with the family members and was able to be there with me. It was great.

I developed a friendship with Shaun Livingston, the point guard for the team. Sometimes, I would get a chance to just chat with him and offer him pointers, some tidbits about what I had learned in my years in the League. Before long, I came to realize that with more practices under our belts together, and all of us healthy, we could be a really good team.

The first 10-day contract expired while we were still on the road. We had just played a game in Philadelphia and we were headed the next day for New York. No one in the Clippers management had come to tell me whether they are re-signing me at this point. I don't even know whether to get on the team plane or not. Should I get on the team plane without a contract? Should I just go back to Seattle and wait until I hear from them? It was another *Twilight Zone* moment—I had absolutely no idea what to do.

Jackie: Ultimately, Doug decided to go on the team plane, even though he didn't yet have the new contract, as we were sure they must have been working on it.

Doug: The next morning at the team brunch, I did sign a second 10-day contract—with the director of Media Relations, even though it was not what I wanted. I wanted to sign for the rest of the season and help the team win games.

Well, after I signed the second 10-day, I noticed that my playing time has all but disappeared. I'm riding the bench and I'm not getting in the game. I'm thinking to myself, "What exactly is going on?"

Jackie: An *L.A. Times* columnist who had interviewed me wrote a column where he described going up to

Clippers' owner Donald Sterling at the game and saying, "You signed Doug Christie—do you know all about him? Do you know all about the stories written about him and his wife? Do you know all about the reality show? Do you know how unusual they are supposed to be?" Well, according to the column, Mr. Sterling hadn't known any of those things about us. And it sure sounded as though he didn't like any of the things he was hearing. Of course, with the time crunch he hadn't had the chance to meet us yet, as we had left Los Angeles with the team to go on a road trip the day after Doug signed. But it worried us, because we didn't want him to think that the old media fodder was true.

And besides, we really liked the *L.A. Times* reporter. He turned out to be a no-nonsense guy with a great sense of humor.

Doug: Keep in mind that when you play basketball, there's five guys and there's only one ball, and there are only forty-eight minutes in a game. So if someone new is coming in and getting minutes, somebody else is losing minutes. It's just a tough situation—one player can only gain playing time at the expense of another.

When I decided not to re-sign with the Clippers at the end of the second 10-day contract, it came as a shock to the media, and that set off a whole new crop of assumptions and lies, but surprisingly, the L.A. media were great. They didn't write the typical satirical stuff that had plagued us for so long. My reason for leaving was that as a professional athlete, I needed stability. It had to be a good fit, not just for the team and for me, but also for my family, too. As I have said before, family comes first!

Jackie: We had really begun to feel welcome again on a team that had huge potential. The city was fantastic, and we were looking forward to being there for a long time.

Doug: I think a lot of people don't know that we ended up donating all of the money from both 10-day contracts to charity. It was a disappointment that it didn't work out with the Clippers. I called Coach Dunleavy just to thank him for the awesome opportunity. I still hold out hope that either this season or next season there will be a team that will not be put off by the negative media my wife and I have been unfortunate enough to receive. It's so crazy. All I want to do is love my wife and my children, be a good husband and a good father, and play basketball. But somehow, in the career I've chosen, there's so much nonsense that gets in the way. That's life, I guess.

There are a lot of other people facing a lot more adversity than we are, so I'm not going to complain. When things like this happen, I remember a comment that a teammate of mine at Pepperdine once made, when I was complaining before practice about how much my feet were hurting. He simply asked, "Doug, what about the guy who has no feet?" Needless to say, I put on my shoes and hit the court saying no more.

~

EIGHT

THE RIGHT SACRIFICE

Jackie: It doesn't matter who you are, where you live, or where you're from. We all have to make sacrifices in life. We all have to make choices, moral and financial. In this chapter, Doug and I want to share our thoughts about how to know which sacrifices to make, and why.

         As we mentioned, some people in Orlando took the position that Doug was not hurt. That he really did not need the surgery. In Orlando, the reporters attacked us. We already told you that story. They said that he was absent from the team and he did not want to be there, and that he could not accept that he had been traded from Sacramento.

Doug: This was the furthest thing from the truth.

Jackie: The truth is Doug did not feel good about taking all of the money when he could not play, so he discussed it with the team management and it was all worked out.

Doug: To some, giving up $1.5 million of salary to do the right thing might be asking a little too much. But not for us. Not because we don't need the money—who doesn't need $1.5 million! Yet the emotional well-being of my family is worth a whole lot more, and I don't even put a monetary figure on that. I was being treated unfairly by some in the sports media and didn't want it to become a distraction to the team, not to mention that I needed surgery. But nonetheless, they were a great group of guys. Besides, my ex-team-mate Hedo from Sacramento was even playing there at the time, too. But giving back that money was the least I could do.

Jackie: This sacrifice will forever be a lesson our children have learned, and they know, no matter what, never compromise your morals and values. Also, put the sanctity of your family first, and there is no amount of money worth the love we share.

Doug: The technical term of what I did is a "buyout" of my contract. Teams are buying contracts out more and more nowadays to clear that money off of their salary cap, so they can sign another player in that spot. What happens is, they take back a sum of the money and pay the player the remaining amount on his contract.

Jackie: I'm so proud of Doug, and the choices he makes. I never feel alone, or like a burden to him, because he truly treats me as his equal. I don't feel threatened by what others think that they can do to us.

Doug: I make sure my wife knows that it is her choice. I tell her, if anything is uncomfortable or stressful for you, just tell me and I will make it go away.

Jackie: Even if it means his favorite sports car. If I feel it's too fast or dangerous, voilà—it's gone!

Doug: No sacrifice is too much for my family.

Jackie: And keep in mind, this is not a one-way street. I will do the same for him. No ifs, ands, or buts. When we are presented with a tough choice, we will sit down and share our feelings on it and then we will decide together the best way to proceed. We never let our wants or needs come before the other's. If I'm all for something and Doug says, "Honey, I don't feel good about this," there is no way I will go forward with it. His comfort is extremely important to me.

Doug: Always make the choice together and take into consideration the other person's feelings.

Jackie: We are sharing with you this story about Doug's contract buyout as an example of how, no matter what monetary value something may have, your family must come first.

Doug: It can't be a tough decision to choose your family, if your heart is truly in it.

Jackie: Always know that by doing what's best for your family, you will also be doing what's best for yourself. The love and respect they will have for you is undeniable.

Doug: As I have said in this book already, basketball is very special to me but what I share with Jackie and how I feel about our family is infinite.

Jackie: We have had to overcome some very tough obstacles in our lives, especially with regard to what the sports media have said about us. So we believe that no matter what bad thing someone may say about you or do to you, always strive to be the bigger person and know in your heart that you made the right choice.

Doug: A sacrifice is most meaningful when it's made for all the right reasons.

Jackie: I agree. Also, we treat everyone with kindness and respect. It may not come back to us in terms of positive treatment from others, but as long as we are doing the right thing, we feel so much better at the end of the day.

Doug: Another example would be this—I am a golfer. I really enjoy a good round of golf with the guys from time to time. But if my wife would rather we go out to lunch or a movie and it's a bright, sunny day (you don't get them all the time in Seattle!), my wife's desires will take precedence over my own.

Jackie: And vice versa. If I want to go shopping and Doug wants to hang out with me at home and watch old movies while the kids go out for ice cream with Grandma, well, you already know my answer! You can shop anytime. Spending quality time with Doug is a hundred percent my choice.

Doug: She'll get her shopping in some other time—you can count on that!

Jackie: It's a girl thing!

Doug: We hope you get the gist of what we are saying to you. A sacrifice for your mate is non-negotiable if you truly strive for Infinite Love.

Jackie: People sometimes ask, "How can I ever get Infinite Love in my life?" And my answer is always the same: "You already have the capacity for it; besides, you come from love. So just build on the foundation you already have." If you don't believe that you can experience Infinite Love, then take this short quiz. You'll be pleasantly surprised by the results—we guarantee it!

The Infinite Love Quiz

1. Would you let your partner eat first if you were both starving?

2. Would you stay home if your partner asked, even though you had plans?

3. Are you grateful for your mate?

4. Would you tell someone "no" if it would make your partner upset if you said "yes"?

5. Do you often say "I love you" to your mate?

6. Do you avoid keeping anger and resentment inside when you have a disagreement with your mate?

7. Do you ask your mate what makes them happy and try to provide it?

8. Would you try to protect your mate at all costs? If they were being attacked?

9. Do you put your mate first?

10. Do you think loving thoughts about your mate often?

If you answered "yes" to any of these questions,
then you are on your way to
I N F I N I T E   L O V E !

NINE

~

YIN

Jackie: A lot of people ask us how we've been able to maintain a solid marriage—what our secrets are.

In this chapter I thought I'd share with you my approach to marriage, and how important it is to put your mate first while respecting yourself and the other person.

As I mentioned earlier, when I was growing up I did not really get a blueprint of a healthy, strong, and committed marriage. But deep inside, I always knew what I wanted and that I had to have it. I knew I wanted someone to love me as much as I would love him, and to treat me as well as I would treat him. We needed to be friends as well as lovers and be able to complete each other's sentences. We had to be SOUL MATES!

Now, mind you, I had never really witnessed this type of love, except for maybe in a movie or on television. But I dreamed about it nonetheless and knew in my mind, even as a little girl with a big heart and dreams of high-fashion, I would find this love or this love would find me.

God is so very good, and He never gives you more than you can handle, as we've said many times. Growing up, I went through some not-too-great relationships on my journey to this dream, yet I never doubted my faith. My spirituality has guided me my whole life. Even though I wasn't perfect, I knew that with a good heart and continuous prayer, all would turn out for the best.

During my childhood, my family spent the summers having picnics and other social gatherings. Even if the food we brought was only sandwiches and soda, the love and closeness was so beautiful, and early on I felt the feeling of being loved. But the love I speak of now, that was something they could not give me. This kind of love would come from my husband one day.

When it comes to marriage, these are my feelings:

1. **Stay committed to the commitment.** By this I mean, that when two people make a commitment to each other, you must uphold that commitment. Protect it and do not waver.

2. **Put your relationship before anything else.** I cannot stress this enough. Your relationship has to be your number one priority.

3. **Give of yourself.** When you give all of yourself to another person, that person will reciprocate. Love and marriage is grand. I don't want to give the impression that it's easy because it's not, but it's yours, and the two of you can make it as good as you want to.

4. **Communication is key.** You both need to

communicate at all times—even if you are tired and talking may be the last thing you feel like doing. At the very least, you can make a promise to your mate to talk about the issue as soon as you are rested and your mind is clear. Sometimes that is the best solution because you can be fully present mentally and communicate more effectively during your conversation. Your being there fully in the moment will make your mate feel the love, commitment, respect, and devotion that you have for the relationship. More times than not, it will also ease the anxiety and tension that is sometimes felt when one person has something to talk about that they feel is important or urgent.

5. **Caring about each other's feelings.** In my mind and heart, this is a big plus. Doug gives me that, with patience, and it means the world to me. In return I make sure to reciprocate, and it nourishes and strengthens our bond.

6. **Trust.** I won't sit here and tell you that trust comes automatically because I wouldn't be telling you the truth. For me, it is something that must be earned and I don't expect someone to trust me right off the bat either. They don't know me, I don't know them, and it just takes time. As you get to know each other, whether it be a coworker, friend, or lover, you can start to build that trust. As you communicate and share yourself with the other person, and them with you, you will begin to develop and cultivate a trust that you can continue to nourish always. And it can't stop when you get married—it must always be something you keep. Trust is the glue that secures your relationship.

Doug:	She is my teacher. I didn't know anything about this until I met Jackie. That is part of why I love her so much. She is easy to love.
Jackie:	Why, thank you, honey!

People struggle sometimes because of images they see on TV, or read in magazines about other folks' relationships. Sometimes they compare their own marriage to the image of other people's marriages as portrayed in the media. This can be very harmful. Your marriage is *your* marriage, and it is special and beautiful. When you open up a magazine and you see a picture of some great-looking couple sitting on the beach in some beautiful tropical place, smiling and cuddling, don't think for a second that they have something you don't. As I said before, your relationship is yours, and you can make it be whatever you want it to be—as strong, loving, committed, and as beautiful as you want. Just try it; you'd be surprised.

Ladies, I am speaking to you right now. Make your relationship a safe haven for your man, a place where he feels like he can talk to you about whatever he wants—anything under the sun. He shouldn't feel like there is any topic that is off limits. If you create a safe place for him, he will open up to you in ways you never imagined.

One thing about guys is that they feel safe when talking with their buddies. Sometimes they are apprehensive to have the same conversation with their mate. So relax, and show him how he can share with you whatever he wants. It will only strengthen the already beautiful relationship you share.

I mean, let's face it, when men are just young boys they are taught to be strong and not to cry when they get an "owie." Young girls are taught that it is okay to cry, and we are cuddled and consoled. So, in addition to the fact that men are, by nature, strong, they are socialized to not show their vulnerable side. Having grown up in a society that does not allow for men's free emotional expression, they may be reluctant to share their feelings with you.

So, it is extremely important to give them the love and support they need in order to trust in you. They need to know that showing you their feelings is acceptable and that you will not scold them for doing so.

Doug cries sometimes and my heart swells because he is the love of my life, my soul mate, and I know that he feels comfortable enough to allow me to share in his feelings. I am truly grateful for that.

7. No stubbornness allowed. There is just not a place in a loving, committed marriage or relationship for this behavior. It not only breaks down the bond, it destroys the trust that you've built together. By being stubborn, you are communicating to your mate that their feelings are not important to you. When you are stubborn, you are being selfish and not putting the relationship first. Always try to live in love with your mate. Never act toward them in a way that you would not want them to act toward you. Really, it all comes back to communication. Communicate, communicate, communicate!

Being devoted to your marriage is the same as being devoted to a church or anything else that is important to you. You do not compromise this devotion. Instead, you ask your mate, "What can I do to make this better? What do you need from me?"

Usually, men just need comfort.

I'd like to share a poem with you that I used to recite when I was growing up. I read it at school one day and it just stuck with me.

> *I do believe that God above*
> *created you for me to love.*
> *He picked you out from all the rest*
> *because he knew that I'd love you best.*
> *And if I die before you do,*
> *I'll meet you at the golden gates*
> *And if you're not there by judgment day,*
> *I'll know you went the other way.*

And lastly, always ask yourself, "What am I bringing to the relationship?" Is it love, loyalty, devotion, and unwavering commitment? Is it romance, thoughtfulness, and trust? If you answer "yes" to all of these questions, then you are doing all the right things to cultivate, stimulate, and nourish your relationship.

TEN

~

YANG

Doug: A man has to know how to let go of his ego and move from "me" to "we" in order to make a marriage work. I'd like to offer some of the thoughts I have on how I've been able to do that.

It starts with respect!

Family first. It's the cornerstone. Jackie and I have a 360-degree circle. We have God, ourselves, our family, and some close friends inside of our circle.

My ego that I had built up over the years was merely a façade, and through my continued search for knowledge of self I have found that you must open your heart and your soul up to your mate and let her in.

As a man, it can sometimes be difficult to step out of your comfort zone, thus becoming vulnerable to your mate. But really, when you love your mate this way, it doesn't take away any of your control. It simply allows you and her to experience true, Infinite Love!

You can experience an intimate connection, a bond, that nothing else can come close to. You must nurture this love you share and cherish it. You've only got one shot! And if you mess this up, often there's no coming back! You always want to keep building and moving forward. If I take good care of my material possessions, why aren't I taking even better care of the spiritual or intangible things in my life—the love, marriage, and family that I enjoy! That's what everything is based on, at least for me.

As a man, you have to give your wife strength. Understand that if you let her be all that she can be, ultimately you'll watch your relationship grow. I mean, let's face it! A woman wants to feel loved, appreciated, and needed! When you help her to feel that way, she can spread her wings and fly.

It's the yin and the yang. The more you are willing to let her in, the more your sensitive side will be able to open up to more growth. I am not ashamed to say that growing up I didn't have these tools. As I now continue to gain them, it is incredible. It took me a very long time to learn that basketball doesn't define me as a man.

What will truly further myself, my family, and my marriage is love. Love is always at the forefront.

In the United States, we do the trade-in thing. When your car is a couple of years old, you trade it in. If your home is a little too small, you knock it down and build a larger one. I think there is something to be said about a nice old car! Besides, I want my wife and me to see the beauty in each other's wrinkled faces one day.

I won't sit here and say that it will all be perfect,

and I won't promise you a rose garden. But I will say it is the best feeling in the world to be faithful to your wife, to love and cherish her and to uphold every vow you made to her.

And what I will promise you is this: every woman wants love, gentlemen! And every woman deserves it. If you give her all that she needs, wants, and deserves, she will shine like the brightest star.

The inner peace it allows her to experience is beyond words and is priceless to her. It takes but mere words to brighten her day, and only a hug to warm her heart. A smile tossed her way will last a long time, and a kiss ... is not just a kiss.

Love her endlessly – Make her know that she is all you need.

Romance – Serenade her in many ways with the kind words you say to her every day.

Faith – Believe in her and in the love that you share. Know that through any ups and downs—you are one.

Trust – Be honest to her and with her about anything and everything, for it is truly the gift of your relationship.

Security – Let her know that she is safe through everything that you do, and that you will stay by her side and will love and protect her always.

Stability – A woman wants to feel stable, and that her home rests upon a solid foundation. Ensure that she knows this.

Comfort – Always put her comfort first, and when she reaches out for you, make sure to be there for her.

And in turn, she will love and take care of you.

And ladies, a man needs and wants to feel respected and loved, too. He wants a woman to be strong in her own special way.

I love that my wife speaks her mind, as she is always coming from love. She only wants the very best for any situation, and it shows. I feel men really want to know that they can trust one hundred percent the woman with whom they have fallen in love. No matter where she is, she will walk with self-respect, dignity, and Infinite Love for her man.

And let's not forget, fellas, there will be the old temptation bug that comes around from time to time. And that's when you just step on it and smash it and hug your beautiful, sexy little lady, because you just avoided what could have been a huge problem later on. Besides, if you're being all the man she needs, and vice versa, then the bug won't even get near the two of you!

Jackie: That's right. And ladies, if it does, then you know what to do, right? You smash it! And then flush it down the toilet! I don't play with that bug comin' in *our* house! We've even installed special screens to keep them outside!

Doug: But seriously, though, never let anything or anyone jeopardize what the two of you share. It can be as beautiful as you want it to be or as strong, but what it can't be is one-sided. So you both must commit to the commitment. I know we mainly are speaking about marriage, but we feel the same way about any relationship. If you're committed to each other, respect and love must be at the center.

~

CREATING BALANCE

Jackie:	A healthy life and a healthy relationship are all about balance, but we live in an unbalanced world. That's true for all of us, no matter what our economic level in life. We are sharing our story so you can see that even the coveted life of the NBA player still has its challenges and disappointments, if you're unwilling to compromise your morals and values, which we will not do.
Doug:	We thought we would share some aspects of our lives even the reality show didn't reveal—about how we strive for balance between the intense demands of work and the equally intense demands of raising a family.
Jackie:	It's intense, all right! For example, Doug's a very patient father to our children and he always spends quality time with them. So I use this time to run errands, do laundry, handle the family business, etc.
Doug:	Maybe some of the celebrities you read about have staffs of people that help them with all of this. But

we like to take care of these responsibilities ourselves, and also spend quality time with our children. We call this "bonding time" in the Christie household.

Jackie: Also, Doug likes to cook and I handle most of the household tasks. That's really the first part of the balancing act. Just getting stuff done for the family—when we put that first, everything else balances out. We always take care of the necessities and then we get to do what we want to do.

Doug: When your mate complements what you're bringing to the table with what she is bringing, that's a winning combination.

Jackie: One which I wouldn't change.

Doug: We are always bonding, working together, growing as a family. No matter what you're doing, you've got to be growing. Using your mind. Maybe there is a new course you want to study, a new subject you want to learn. You can always find the time if you want to.

Jackie: I try to be organized. I'm big on making lists. It will help to get the day going in a productive way and allows you to see your progress as you are able to cross off the task that you complete, and to feel good at the end of the day.

Doug: Even though it may seem that twenty-four hours is just not enough time to do all the things you want to, if you set goals and write down your tasks, you can then decide on the road map to take to achieve getting it all done.

Jackie: We include our children in a lot of the household things we have going on. Instead of saying, "Go sit down and we'll do it," we say, "Can you help

	Mommy or Daddy with this or that?" And they, of course, are delighted.
Doug:	Unless their favorite TV show is on.
Jackie:	Yes, that's true!
Doug:	But the moral of this story is this: you must put the time into your relationship with your mate and into your family, for this is the foundation of love, the foundation of finding balance.
Jackie:	I always make sure to ask my husband if there is anything he needs or wants from me, so I can make sure he is always full of my love and support for him. I also do the same with our children, for that teaches them how to love, how to give of themselves, and how to treat their mate.
Doug:	We teach them by example. The travel that comes along with a basketball career is extensive. Because we are such a close-knit family, our mother lives with us year-round. Even though Jackie travels with me at times, our kids still have Grandma there and that gives them stability. Also, they have bonded with their grandmother and feel secure in her care.
Jackie:	We don't allow anyone to baby-sit our children except family. It's best for us this way.
Doug:	Our children prefer Grandma.
Jackie:	And we have high phone bills because we are calling them ten times a day when we are away. We are always connecting with each other and it gives us all a feeling of closeness and love.
Doug:	Finding balance simply means putting everything in your life that's important to you first.
Jackie:	I agree.
Doug:	Really, every relationship is unique, but Infinite Love is universal.

Jackie: We were always careful not to tell the NBA or anyone else how to portray marriage. We were never on a crusade—"Be like us!"

Doug: I stay focused on what I'm doing. I don't get involved in anything that is not beneficial to me and to my family.

Jackie: That goes both ways. The importance of family and making sure you're taking care of business in every aspect will give you the peace of mind to find your balance.

Doug: In life, you will run into some ups and downs, but when you have a strong support system, they seem to be only small things, as you're not fighting them alone.

Jackie: For the wife of an NBA player, it also takes patience, strength, and courage and commitment to not just your marriage but also to being the cornerstone. You will spend many a night alone, but that's what telephones are for, ladies! To call our hubbies anytime we want to. And believe me, I do. There will also be times when you are pushed aside by an eager fan going after the almighty autograph from your mate. You have to just smile and step aside because, really, they have a right to have access to the very public figure you married.

When you have that special someone in your life, just make sure you're being all to them that you want them to be to you. Together, by putting each other first, you will find your balance.

TWELVE

~

THE REALITY BEHIND REALITY TV

Jackie: The one thing that having a reality show teaches you is that whatever you see on a reality show ... often has to be taken with a grain of salt. That's a lesson you could say we learned the hard way!

Doug: I was practicing one day at our home in Seattle, when Jackie had a conversation with the people who became the producers of our show. They called and asked if we would be interested in our own reality show, and said that they had followed our story and knew we had something special. You see, the husband of the lady on the phone was also an NBA player, so she had firsthand knowledge about us.

When Jackie told me what the person had in mind, my first reaction was firm and absolute—no! Absolutely not! They'll kill us!

Jackie: We talked, and ultimately we decided that it would give us a chance to show people how we really are, how we really live. So we signed on, and they started shooting. At the time, Doug was playing for the

Sacramento Kings. Reports were everywhere—"Finally, we'll get a chance to see just how whipped and henpecked Doug Christie really is," they wrote.

We were assured over and over again that the show would be positive. And then some individuals involved in the show called me one day with a teeny-weeny little change. (I did most of the phone conferences, because Doug was busy with the team obligations.) They said that instead of the show being spontaneous and unrehearsed, in other words, a real reality show, it would be scripted.

Doug: Imagine that—a scripted reality show!

Jackie: They actually said to me, "Since people already see you as overbearing and crazy, let's take advantage of that image!"

They were *not* off to the right start with me. I must admit, I was not happy at all about this new idea.

They said, for example, "You guys go to a restaurant. Jackie, you'll go to the restroom, and then we'll send some girls over to Doug. When you come out of the restroom, you'll see them standing there, and then you'll attack them! Doesn't that sound great?"

Doug: No, it did not sound great.

Jackie: It was appalling. One of the main reasons we were doing the show was to squash the misconceptions people have about us. So I said, "No, we had an expectation that this would be a real reality show. I'm sorry, this is not what we're going to do. It'll just make matters worse."

They said they wanted to have me look domineering, and that they'd then turn it around by the end of the season and have people absolutely loving me. I'll never forget the next words they said: "Well, that's the show!"

"Then we don't have a show!" I responded, and that was that. I worried for a few minutes that I had just ruined our only chance to show everyone the truth—besides, it was a terrific network, too.

Well, I prayed about it, then told Doug, and he said, "Babe, I'm so sorry they said that to you, but you did the right thing. They didn't mean it personally, I don't think. This is also a business and they need to get ratings. No biggie. We will move on. If it's meant to be, then the right fit will come."

We were fortunate enough to find a home at BET, which licensed the footage that was already shot. From the start, they were good to us and treated us right. From its first season, the show captured who we are.

BET had a second channel, BETJ (BET Jazz), and in our time slot the producers told us that viewership was up four hundred percent over their previous offering. Bringing a show with a celebrity athlete was the way BET sent a strong message in order to aid the re-launch of that network. We did red carpets and events, all kinds of things. We did a press tour around the country, and we got an overwhelmingly positive response for the show.

Doug: I was concerned about going into the show, considering everything that had already been said about us. Whatever we did, I thought would get spun the wrong way. I wondered if they were going to make the whole thing into something negative. Ultimately, though, I figured this would be a good thing—a way for people to judge for themselves. That way, they'd be able to see that all the things that had been said about us were just not true.

Jackie: We got no negative feedback personally whatsoever about the show, except a few people asking when was I going to go crazy on someone. I found that question funny! But of course, there are some haters out there who will say some derogatory things, and they wrote a few silly blogs. That's life, I guess.

Doug: It's like anything else—you might hear things about people you don't know, but once you see how they treat each other, the truth comes out. The show helped us dispel the lies that had been spread about us. We did a show on the trade from Sacramento to Orlando, where we're packing up to leave. That was a very emotional show. We did another one on my surgery, to show that I was really hurt, contrary to some of the media reports. Everyone got to see the entire operation, through the healing process. There's a lot of seriousness to our life, but there's also a lot of lightheartedness. We enjoy having fun.

Jackie: Doug did a dance and people got to see his silly side, how he deals with the kids. At times, we would completely forget that the cameras were there.

Doug: On one of the episodes, we went to Jamaica. My friend Tyrone was going with us, but he managed to come to the airport without either a passport or a birth certificate. I was like, "Tyrone, don't you realize that Jamaica isn't part of the United States?" We ended up having to leave him in Miami. When he finally arrived, it was on the last day of our trip—and he jumped in the pool, fully clothed. It was so funny!

Jackie: We try hard not to sugarcoat anything or depict ourselves in any way contrary to reality.

Doug: The main thing I liked about the show was that it said you could be an athlete or whatever and still love your wife and family. It wasn't that big a deal for me to see myself on the show, because I was used to seeing myself in game films. It was new to see me acting like me. That was different.

Jackie: It was so exciting the first time we saw each episode, because we never knew what we were going to see. They didn't tell us what they were going to use. You have to let them edit it and produce the finished show.

Doug: Half the time, I'd be pulling my T-shirt up over my head whenever I saw myself on the screen, going, "I can't believe I did that," or "I can't believe I said that."

Jackie: It's okay, babe. It's all in good fun.

    These shows are called reality shows because unless they're scripted, like the one we turned down, they really are about reality! If you let them, they'll have a camera in your bedroom at five a.m. when you wake up. So we'd tell them, we'll be up at eight. But we'd actually get up at six so we could shower and dress before the cameras arrived! It was our little inside joke. Also, one of the other things we tried to pay attention to was our language. Sometimes when you're excited or angry about something, you might swear. And then I'll think, "Oh, no—that's not the message for my kids ... or any kids if they watch!" Of course, the cameras would capture all of that.

Doug: They get it all!

Jackie: This may sound surprising, but it wasn't intrusive to have the cameras around. We knew what we were getting into, so we weren't incredibly surprised.

	They'd shoot, and then they'd leave. After a while, the kids would be asking, "When are the camera guys coming back?"
Doug:	Or something would happen and you'd say, "Where are the cameras? They should have gotten that!" The weird thing is that they follow you everywhere in the house except into the bathroom. It's very hard to hide from them. If that's what you're trying to do!
Jackie:	You try to take the phone to another room for privacy ... and then there's another camera on you over there.
Doug:	I would tell my friends, "I'm five-oh"—that meant "I'm the police"—whenever I wore the mic.
Jackie:	Sometimes I'd write Doug a note and hope that he got it before the cameramen did! Other times, I'd turn off my mic so I could tell Doug something in private, and the sound guys would start yelling, "Hey, your mic is off!"
Doug:	I'd be like, "Maybe I need a new battery!"
Jackie:	Then they brought in remote mics.
Doug:	That's because I took the batteries out of my clip-on mic. They figured out what I had done. They were saying, "Where's the battery?" It was hilarious—we would laugh and so would the camera crew. We had so much fun doing the show.
Jackie:	The show started while we were still in Sacramento, and the team was great about it. We were told that the NBA had given the producers the green light to film during games. Maybe they recognized that we did have a positive message and that it had been filtered unfairly by some of the sports media.

Doug: The reality show, overall, was a great experience for our family. We let the public see who we are. We've gotten tons of e-mails that read things like, "Before I watched the show, all I knew about you is what I read. Now I see that you guys have been treated very unkindly." I feel honored that in my lifetime I've been able not just to play basketball at the highest level, which is a huge privilege and enormous fun. On top of that, we've been able to help carry the message of Infinite Love to the maximum number of people, through our show and television appearances ... and now, we hope, through this book.

#1

THIRTEEN

~

WILL YOU MARRY ME ... AGAIN?

Doug: I have now asked Jackie to be my wife a total of twelve times. We get married every year—we have an actual wedding ceremony, and I wouldn't change it for anything in the world. My lovely bride just keeps bringing me to my knees with her inner and outer beauty. She is the true love of my life.

Jackie: And Doug is my knight in shining armor!

Doug: Every year that we have gotten married, we've had a theme to our wedding.

And each year, the number of guests varies as well.

Jackie: Some of the weddings have been huge and others small and intimate, but all have been filled with Infinite Love.

Doug: I second that, baby!

Jackie: Our first wedding, we were engaged on Saturday and man and wife on Tuesday. I wore a sexy black cocktail dress and white pearls. Doug wore the traditional black tux. Pink and white were our accent colors, and

gorgeous red roses made up the bridal bouquet. We had sixty-five guests in attendance.

Doug: Our second wedding was much bigger, with a hundred and fifty guests. And our colors were traditional as well—with Jackie wearing a beautiful white princess-style wedding dress with a long train and beaded bodice. She had the glow of a happy bride, and again she brought tears of joy to my eyes.

Jackie: For our third wedding, we were on a cruise ship in the Caribbean, and it was magnificent. I wore a long, midnight-blue dress with the prettiest embroidery all over it that I'd ever seen. Doug wore a pale blue two-piece suit and looked ultra handsome. He had that suntanned glow to his skin, and I remember his hazel eyes were stunning.

Doug: Oh, yes. On our fourth wedding, we decided to get married in downtown Seattle at our favorite hotel and getaway, the Four Seasons, now called the Fairmont Hotel. We booked the Presidential Suite and invited close friends and family to join us. We feasted on seafood and lemon meringue pie. It was delicious! Once everyone left, including Grandma,

#3

who took our kids with her, we had our fourth honeymoon. We enjoyed two days of private bliss.

Jackie: Okay, honey! Stay on track! On our fifth wedding, we were in Jamaica, our most favorite spot to vacation in the world. We got married by ourselves, with the minister officiating as usual. We were staying in an oceanfront hotel with one of the most stunning views imaginable, and we said "I do" once more.

Doug: On our sixth wedding, we got married in Seattle, at our favorite hotel, once again, because the time before was so special. Only this time, we had a private wedding—just the two of us, and our minister to re-marry us. For the second time, it was beautiful.

Jackie: On our seventh wedding, we were married in a very private, romantic ceremony with us writing our own vows to go along with traditional ones. It was very special as well, because Doug's agent is also an ordained minister, and so for this wedding, we asked him to officiate, which he did. It strengthened our bond with him as well.

Doug: On our eighth wedding, we got married on the soil of our new property we bought in order to build our dream home. We wore fatigues to pay tribute to the battle we had fought with all the sports media for us making a stand to be faithful to each other and to forsake one another for no one and for nothing.

Jackie: The ninth wedding was very nice—we married inside the foundation of the structure, with just us and our kids in our soon-to-be-completed home. We wore overalls and yellow hardhats to pay tribute to our home being built.

#8

Doug: The tenth wedding was grand. We again married at
           our home, as it was just completed that same year.
           We had all of the guests wearing black—the men in
           traditional tuxedos, and the ladies in formal black
           gowns. Rose petals were sprinkled all about the foyer,
           and it was a special occasion. It was also shown on
           our reality show.

Jackie: Our eleventh wedding was beautiful. We married in
           Seattle with just Doug and me, our kids, the minister,
           and the photographer—an intimate, simple affair to

capture another of our beautiful memories on our special day once again.

Doug: It is so very exciting to plan our weddings; it's also a way of sharing our special love with others as well. People say to us all the time, "We really love what the two of you are doing. Now we're going to get married again, too!" They ask, "How do you keep the fire alive?" And we both respond this way: "You have to put logs on it!" In other words, always nourish your marriage. Do not starve it. You can use the analogy that if the fire just burns and logs are not added, it will eventually burn out. That's the same for marriage. When we marry each year, we are saying to each other, "My love for you is strong. My desire to be your spouse is steadfast. And you are the love of my life."

Jackie: Our children always say to us, "Mommy and Daddy, when I grow up I'm going to marry my mate every

#10

year, too!" So in a sense, we have started a family tradition. And lastly, the special day two people share when they marry doesn't have to be once or in twenty-five years. It can be as often as the two of you would like ... and all throughout the year the Infinite Love will shine through.

~

FOURTEEN

Hobbies for Two

Doug: I started collecting antique cars in 1997. The first one I acquired was my dad's old 1966 T-Bird; it was red on red before I completely restored it and now it is steel grey in color, and it also has the sliding steering wheel. Antique cars are special. They have their own personality. They can even bring back memories just by their smells. This is what happened to me every time I got in the back of my dad's '66 Thunderbird. I would get in and that old car smell would hit me.

        When I grew up, I asked my dad if I could restore it for him and he agreed and my hobby began! I still remember when it arrived on the tow truck ...

Jackie: What a sight!

Doug: I knew then, I had my work cut out for me!

Jackie: It sure was!

Doug: Aw babe, it wasn't that bad. Anyway, first things first. The car needed a complete overhaul—seeing how possums were living in the engine before it was brought to us! But as soon as it was done I was thrilled. From the paint job to the ride, it was magnificent! It also had special meaning to me—having been my dad's car when I was a boy.

The second car I got was a 1966 Mustang. I call it my "Black Beauty"!

Jackie: Excuse me! I thought that was my pet name, honey!

Doug: It is, babe! Come on now!

Okay, back to my '66 Mustang. When I got it I was overjoyed, as it was one of my dream cars. It is a convertible, and by the time I restored it, it shined like a black pearl.

Jackie: Now that's more like it!

Doug: It's also very fast, with a 302 engine and torque thrust wheels.

Jackie: Remember earlier in the book I mentioned that if Doug had a car that was too fast and I was uncomfortable, voilà—it was gone? Well, not this one! This one's special!

Doug: The third one I got was a Christmas gift I received while playing in Toronto. My wife located it from a car collector in Oregon, and it truly was a dream come true! The '57 Chevy is the grandfather of my antique car collection. It also has a Corvette engine and billet aluminum rims. It's a real gem!

Jackie: Yes, and it was my favorite until SHE came along ...

Doug: That would be our fourth addition—my wife's turquoise blue '56 T-Bird. She saw it on TV once in a Nicolas Cage movie and fell in love with it, so I found one for her and gave it to her for our fifth wedding anniversary.

Jackie: I cried when I saw it. I was just so overwhelmed by its beauty. Now I too have become a collector and we have yet another thing in common!

Doug: Yes, babe, we do.

Jackie: I have a special hobby as well—reading. I love, love, love to read, not only for the added knowledge but also for all the wonderful discoveries I can find inside books!

I come from a long line of readers and I personally decided long ago that reading is one of my favorite pastimes. I have learned a great deal by just picking up a book—books have a lot of great tips and advice.

We strongly encourage our kids to read as well. Doug taught all of them how to read. Sometimes Doug and I will have a reading night when we just relax and read and then share our stories and compare notes. We have also taught ourselves a great deal by reading.

Another of my favorite pastimes is online shopping. Let me share with you some cool destinations that I enjoy ...

JACKIE'S FAVORITE ONLINE SHOPPING SITES

Designer handbags for a fraction of the retail cost
Bluefly.com
SmartBargains.com
Overstock.com

Designer shoes
Zappos.com
Nordstrom.com
Shoes.com

Popular clothing/accessories
ShopKitson.com
ShopIntuition.com
eLUXURY.com

Music
iTunes.com

Variety at a great price
Target.com

Sportswear
Adidas.com
Nike.com
Eastbay.com

Books
Amazon.com
BarnesandNoble.com

Doug: My favorite website is google.com because every-
         thing can be found by just typing in what you are
         looking for in the search box.

         Also, in addition to shopping online, we really
         enjoy a day out at the fabric store finding unique
         fabric to create pieces for our clothing line.

Jackie: It is a wonderful thing to sit and collaborate together
         about fashion.

Doug: That's another passion in common!

Jackie: With both of us being from Seattle, we really love
         seafood, and fishing is another hobby Doug really
         enjoys. My favorite part of a fishing trip is the quiet
         relaxation of being out on the lake with him at six
         a.m. waiting for the fish to bite ...

Doug: Fishing is one of life's special treasures! As the
         Chinese proverb goes, and as my father often said to
         me: "Give a man a fish and you feed him for a day.
         Teach a man to fish and you feed him for a lifetime."

         Now going to Jamaica, this is something we
         never tire of. We have a very special place in Montego
         Bay that we call our home away from home.

Jackie: Half Moon Bay is a beautiful resort and we have
         been there quite a few times. We usually take along a
         few close friends, as the villa home we rent has five
         bedrooms, and we just eat, relax, golf, and have a
         blast.

Doug: The people are like family to us. We always request
         the same group to cook our delicious meals and we
         always enjoy each other's company.

Jackie: I get to sleep as much as I want while Doug goes
         golfing almost every day. We go into the city and we

are like kids in a candy shop. It's always an adventure. We find great bargains and unique gifts to bring home—from music to clothing to authentic Jamaican artwork.

We could go on and on about this favorite vacation spot of ours.

Doug: Simply put, we love it ...

Jackie: We hope you enjoyed this chapter on our beloved hobbies and some of our other favorite things to do. Being able to enjoy them together makes them even more fun! We encourage you and your mate to try mixing some of your hobbies together into something you can both enjoy. This will allow you to spend even more special time with each other!

FIFTEEN

~

THE MESSAGE

Jackie: We hope that by now you've received our message—that we're not going to compromise our values for the sake of others' misgivings. If there's just one message that you take from our book, I hope it's this: it's better to stand firm on your beliefs than to compromise your values. This is just as true in relationships as it is in work and every other aspect of life. If the person isn't the right person, and you know that in your heart, maybe it's time to move on. If your work situation is causing you more pain and grief than any job is worth, then you have to reassess: "Could God have something else or someone else better for me?"

On the other hand, I don't mean this as an excuse to cut and run. This is *not* about saying, "He said something mean," or "She said something mean and I'm outta here." Or, "My boss yelled at me so I'm done with this job." Life isn't about quitting. It's about making the absolute best of the situation you have at hand, and then really communing with your heart to find out if what you're doing is in keeping with your truest values.

We talked earlier about how we live in an era of throwaway marriages. But we also live in an era of throwaway values. People just toss their values aside if they think a good opportunity is coming along—a relationship, a job, a place to live, whatever. I know some people may think that since I'm married to Doug, and he's an NBA player, I don't have the same problems and issues. Well, I'll be the first to tell you it's not the case. My life, more than most, is under a microscope and I am judged unfairly by some in the sports media ... just for being his wife and loving him, and him for loving me.

I also know we have mentioned quite a bit about the sports media taking shots at us. But there's a reason for that. Many in the sports genre have purposely tried to belittle us. And that's not the case with the entertainment media, who have been very fair and not judgmental in any way.

Just today, as we were writing this chapter, we did an interview with a major national sports talk radio program that had been seeking for some time to have us on the air. But no sooner had they introduced us, than they started in with the same old stuff. "Doug, does the fact that people perceive you as 'whipped' overshadow your great NBA career?" And then, after they asked Doug whether he still wanted to play (of course he does!), they asked me, "Jackie, will you let him?" You just have to shake your head and ask why it has to be this way. We stand for marriage and commitment; we'll take the criticism if we can get our message out.

I hope throughout this book that you've felt like you're getting to know the real Doug and me better, and that you can form your own opinion now that we have spoken in our words—unedited and very raw. I hope that what you've learned in this book counterbalances some of the things you may have heard about us, in media coverage or interviews like the one we did today.

We invite you into our world to experience the Infinite Love that we truly share. And I would just like to add that everyone has to make decisions. So just always try to make the best one for you and your family.

Most of us live lives where we just accept whatever is handed to us. "How much can you guys take?" That's really the question the world asks us all. "How much abuse, negativity, and disappointment can you take?" Well, I believe the real answer is that we shouldn't have to take any. I'm not talking about the occasional pebble-in-the-shoe problems that we all have from time to time. What I am saying is that when we compromise our values for the sake of expediency, for the sake of what looks glamorous or cool, we're just setting ourselves up for bigger problems down the road.

Let's say we had stayed with a certain team. What cost would we—and our children—have paid by accepting the terms that were offered there? I'm not talking about the financial terms, the numbers in Doug's contract. I'm talking about the emotional abuse—the fact that I was warned when we first arrived that my reputation preceded me. As long as I remained passive and tried to get along, the media would discuss me in a positive light. But if I wasn't willing to go along with it, the media would return to their old habits about me and paint a malicious picture that had nothing to do with reality.

If we tolerated that, if we had shown by our actions that that sort of behavior was acceptable and they could get away with doing those things, where would it have gone next? And where would it have gone after that? If you know Doug, you know how much he loves to play basketball. You know how much he loves to play and compete, and you know how proud and happy he is that he's been able to spend fourteen years playing at the highest level in the world, in the National Basketball Association, with and against some of the greatest players ever—Chris Webber, Dwayne Wade, LeBron James, Tracy McGrady, Michael Jordan, Kobe Bryant, Allen Iverson, Shaquille O'Neal. And of course the list goes on.

Doug: I have had the privilege of experiencing my boyhood dream come true, a dream that I share with practically every young man in America, to compete and succeed at the highest levels of sport. But as important as that dream is and remains to me, I wasn't willing to follow it at the cost of deep emotional pain to myself, my wife, or our children.

Jackie: I would love, honor, and respect my husband no matter what decision he had made with regard to any team he played for—even this past season with Seattle. But when it comes to gratitude, my cup runneth over when I think about the sacrifice that Doug was willing to make in order to spare his family from any further emotional abuse.

Doug has two dreams—one is to return to the NBA—and find the right fit—and the other is to continue to be the husband and father he loves to be, the man he is proud to have become. He had to make a choice, and he opted for preserving his family instead of prolonging his career. But again, acting on your values means choosing one thing you want over another, and that's what Doug has done.

There comes a time in every athlete's career when he can no longer compete at the professional level. Whether that happens for Doug at age thirty-six or forty or forty-four, there will be a day when he can no longer play the game at that level. But marriage and family—that lasts for the rest of his life. Doug wasn't willing to accept short-term pleasure at the expense of long-term happiness.

Doug: The thing about my wife is that she's still the same girl I married—beautiful, loving, funny, intelligent, witty, charming, the whole package. I'm not a boisterous person by nature. Maybe that reflects my upbringing as an only child. Back then, as I've said, it was just me and my mom. I didn't have a big family as Jackie did. But what's important to me is not whether I'm the life of the party or whether I'd just be happier sitting at home, reading a book or working on my jump shot. What matters to me most is that I knew what I wanted and I was fortunate enough to have found Jackie. Yes, even as a child I always harbored the dream of playing in the NBA. I'd be lying if I told you otherwise. But the dream that I never admitted to anyone, and barely even acknowledged to myself, was that I wanted the happy, stable marriage and family that had unfortunately eluded both my parents and Jackie's. As I've said repeatedly throughout this book, I knew what I wanted but I didn't know how to get there. I've been blessed with many great coaches and teachers in the game of basketball, from my high school coach Mel Williams through Rick Adelman of the Sacramento Kings. But my greatest teacher, my greatest coach, and my greatest source of inspiration is Jackie, because she knew how to get the lesson across to a somewhat resistant student. Jackie embodies love because, like love, she was patient and kind. She didn't have to stick around waiting for me. With all of her qualities (and not to mention good looks!), she could have gotten any man. But she knew what she wanted, and what she wanted was me! I used to have a hard time believing that, but I know it in my heart now that we were destined to be soul mates. And so we are, despite everything you might have heard about us!

If you've ever been to a redwood forest, then you know what it's like to stand in awe of those tall, proud, elegant trees that soar straight into the sky, offering those at ground level a beautiful canopy of shade. The question that visitors sometimes have when they look at the redwoods is how trees that huge could be supported by roots that would have to be gargantuan in their own right. How could redwoods stand so close together if they need such deep roots to provide stability?

The surprising answer is that the roots of

redwood trees intertwine under the soil, year after year, decade after decade. The intertwining of their roots is the source of their stability and strength and allows them to grow unbowed toward the heavens.

That's what Infinite Love is all about. It's the intertwining of roots below the surface. When you see a happily married couple, you're seeing two redwoods growing side by side, and if they are a family, then you're seeing a grove of them, walking tall together. And what allows them that closeness, be it the marriage or the family, is that intertwining and intermingling of roots. That's what a lot of the reporters and broadcasters might not have been able to see when they were writing about us and saying crazy things about us. They didn't see the intertwining of roots, a process that brings us closer and closer together, day after day, year after year, and, we pray, decade after decade.

If Jackie and I had lacked those roots, that mutual foundation of love and support, we might not have withstood the tough times, the public criticism and ridicule, the accusations, jealousies of others, all the petty nonsense that we have endured. (I'd use a stronger word than "nonsense," but I'm hoping that maybe your kids will read this book, too, one day!) But our faith in God, the depth of our roots, and the degree to which they were intertwined allowed us to weather those storms, and here we are, still standing tall.

I won't lie. I'd love to be back in the NBA. But not at the price of my wife's or my serenity. If I thought the money I had to give back to Dallas and

Orlando from my contract when I couldn't play for those teams were high amounts, they look like chump change compared to the cost of putting Jackie through any more nonsense. I know that in this book we've taken a firm position and sometimes even a harsh stance toward some of the people, institutions, and broadcasters that have sought to hurt us. But once again, as the expression goes, a lie never reaches old age. The purpose of this book has not been to paint myself as a malcontent or someone who is ungrateful for the opportunities that playing ball in the NBA have given me. Far from it. We're just trying to set the record straight, on behalf of ourselves, on behalf of our family, and even on behalf of the institution of marriage. We want people to know that marriage can be beautiful. That marriage is beautiful! We never sought out positions for ourselves as role models in the African American community for a strong and healthy marriage, but this is obviously the role into which God has thrust us. We welcome the opportunity to tell everyone that marriage rocks, that marriage is cool, that you really can get from where you are not just to the wedding altar but to "happily ever after."

I know lots of people who have never married and I know lots of people who have married and divorced. But I'm the only person I know who has married the same woman *twelve times* … and counting! As my wife says, it's hard to plan a divorce when you're busy planning a wedding. So that's what we'll be doing. You can count on the fact that every July 8th, we'll be there with our friends and family, the minister, our vows and our commitment to each other and to what we stand for with the time we've been allotted on Earth.

We were never looking for trouble, and yet somehow trouble found us. I think that's true for a lot of people. Adversity is just a test life gives you so that you can find out what you're made of. Dating is like the regular season in the NBA. A committed relationship is like the playoffs ... and marriage is like the NBA Finals! Maybe the whole world isn't watching your marriage, but your kids are. Your family is. Your friends are. Your community is. Maybe every move you make isn't tracked in the sports media, which is our lot in life, one that we didn't seek out but one that we understand and accept. But we're all role models for the kids down the block, the couple in the next car over, our coworkers, let alone our family and friends. The great golfer Lee Trevino says, "What you take with you is what you leave behind." My kids wouldn't care one way or the other about me if I left behind a record as a solid NBA player but a legacy as a poor husband and father. Before I met Jackie, I knew what I didn't want. I knew what that looked like. Until I met her, I had never known that what I wanted was out there for me.

Whoever you are, whatever you're going through, I believe your heart's deepest desire is waiting for you, too. Nobody's going to tell you that the road will be easy, because that's not how life is. You don't need me to tell you that life is full of highs and lows—you can discover that anywhere from the Bible to Dr. Seuss! My message is that you should never give up hope or faith in yourself or in the possibility of Infinite Love. I'd rather stand tall, like a redwood, with my wife and children than cringe dealing with any organization that condones inappropriate and unacceptable behavior on the part of its employees toward the woman I love. In the abstract, it might sound like a hard choice to give up an opportunity to play basketball with any team by balancing the experience of playing against the things that you've read about in this book. It was never a hard choice. When you know and love your soul mate, it's the easiest thing in the world to put them ahead of everything else.

So that's my message to the men reading this book—stick your ego in your back pocket. Maybe it's making you look bigger than you are, but it's hard to reconcile fronting with love. Let that special someone see the real you. Let yourself see the real you. You might just be surprised by what you find.

Jackie: This whole book has been a conversation between Doug and me, but now we want you to join the conversation. We'd love to hear from you. You can visit us at www.InfiniteLovePublishing.com. We want to hear how you're taking the message of Infinite Love into your life.

Doug: Jackie handles the e-mails. I'm not much of a computer guy.

Jackie: I print them out, though, and then Doug reads them. So we'll both see what you have to say. We hope this book has served its purpose—to give you a true picture of the two of us, of marriage, and of what it takes to succeed. Doug and I wish you and everyone in your life all of the blessings ... of Infinite Love.

Acknowledgments

To Tyrone (Tye), my friend for life—Respect!

To William (stinker), my brother and mentor, thank you for the knowledge!

To Glen (Pete), my coach and friend, thanks for the cakes!

To my best friend Shelly (Shell), thanks for always being there.

To my best friend Tamika, thanks for the good times!

To my best friend Patricia (Tricia). Girl, go to charm school!

To Maryse, thanks for your belief in us.

To Coach Tom Asbury, thanks for the opportunity!

To Johnny Ray (Jr.), thanks for all the years!

To Mel Williams, for your belief in me.

To Michael Levin, our co-author and friend, we thank you for your belief, support, and undying commitment to helping us convey our message to the world!

We also want to thank our wonderful publishing team: Dotti Albertine, book designer; Brookes Nohlgren, copyeditor; Bill Frank, distribution consultant; Mike Brown and Roger Kindley, attorneys; Terrie Barna, typist; and Nicole Rhoton, Michael Levin's outstanding assistant.

Footprints

One night I had a dream—
I dreamed I was walking along the beach with the Lord
And across the sky flashed scenes from my life.
For each scene I noticed two sets of footprints,
One belonged to me and the other to the Lord.
When the last scene of my life flashed before me,
I looked back at the footprints in the sand.
I noticed that many times along the path of my life,
There was only one set of footprints.
I also noticed that it happened
at the very lowest and saddest times in my life.
This really bothered me and I questioned the Lord about it.
"Lord, you said that once I decided to follow you,
you would walk with me all the way,
but I have noticed that during the most
troublesome times in my life,
there is only one set of footprints.
I don't understand why in times when I needed you most,
You should leave me."
"My precious, precious child,
I love you and I would never, never leave you
during your times of trial and suffering.
When you saw only one set of footprints,
It was then that I carried you."

— MARY STEVENSON

www.InfiniteLovePublishing.com

www.InfiniteLovePublishing.com